S0-CFM-817

ICE HOCKEY RULES
IN PICTURES

Edited by ROBERT SCHARFF

Illustrated by John McDermott

Foreword by
CLARENCE S. CAMPBELL
PRESIDENT OF THE NATIONAL HOCKEY LEAGUE

GROSSET & DUNLAP (H) Publishers · New York

ICE HOCKEY RULES IN PICTURES

© 1967 BY GROSSET & DUNLAP, INC.

ALL RIGHTS RESERVED

PUBLISHED SIMULTANEOUSLY IN CANADA

LIBRARY OF CONGRESS CATALOG CARD NUMBER: 67-23794

PRINTED IN THE UNITED STATES OF AMERICA
Second Printing

FOREWORD

In the current explosion of interest and enthusiasm for the game of Hockey, spurred on by the great "Expansion" of the National Hockey League to six additional metropolitan areas in the United States extending from coast-to-coast, the appearance of this excellent presentation of its Playing Rules is both timely and welcome.

Basically Hockey is a simple game for the neophyte spectator to understand and enjoy. Unlike some other sports, which require a good preliminary grounding in the basic rules in order to have any real appreciation of what is happening, Hockey is so simple to understand that a first-time spectator has no difficulty in comprehending its main features after one evening's exposure with or without instruction or comment from anyone. This is one of its greatest attractions and advantages.

However, on closer and more frequent acquaintance the new spectator discovers that there are in fact a very substantial number of rules and interpretations which should be known and understood if he is to develop his "expertise" in the sport and there is a special vernacular which is constantly used by the real aficionados which should be mastered if he is to converse knowledgeably about the game.

To illustrate how time has expanded the rule book, here are a few pertinent facts. The earliest code (pre 1900) consisted of 18 short sections which could be printed on less than four pages. By 1917 (when the NHL was founded) there were 30 sections covering eight small pages. Today there are 84 sections with many sub-sections which fill 64 closely printed pages along with further diagrams and illustrations!

Unhappily the printed word is not always capable of conveying to the reader a clear impression of the correct import of any particular rule and it is the solution of this problem which this excellent book provides through the medium of a very complete set of excellent sketches and diagrams illustrating many facets of the game and its terms.

It also contains an extensive glossary of these terms with precise definitions. For the college hockey fan it identifies the principal differences between the amateur code employed in United States colleges and the code which governs play in the National Hockey League. For those who wish to delve more deeply into the exact text of the professional code, pertinent NHL Playing Rules 1967-68 are included.

This splendid manual has much to offer to the beginner and the old-timer alike. It is written in attractive style and beautifully illustrated. It will prove to be a useful ready reference for anyone having any interest, whether active or latent, in the sport.

It is indeed a welcome addition to the literature of the Game.

C. S. Campbell
President
National Hockey League

CONTENTS

INTRODUCTION TO ICE HOCKEY

Hockey—a game of rousing speed, spectator appeal and color—is the fastest team sport in the world. It is of Canadian origin, derived from the ancient European game of bandy and refined from the French field game of "hoquet." Field hockey, and the related field games of "hurley" and "shinny" involving the same stick-and-object principle, evidently came to Canada with the British garrisons stationed there. With long seasons when lake and harbor ice was available for skating, it was only natural that these games should soon be played on skates on the open ice surfaces. Field hockey sticks were used, and the object hit and passed was a rubber ball. There was no limit to the number of players on a side. The first recorded game of this type was reported in Kingston, Ontario, in 1878.

The first set of rules was devised by a graduate and a student at McGill University in Montreal, W. F. Robertson and R. F. Smith. They combined some of the rules of field hockey with those of rugby, with nine players on a side. Regular goal cages were set up and goalkeepers introduced; instead of a ball, a flat puck was used; finally, the playing positions were given definite names.

Hockey came to the United States at the turn of the century with team strength reduced to seven. In 1911 the team strength was set at its present limit of six. Today, thousands of Canadians and Americans play and millions watch hockey games each winter. The sport is also very popular in Japan, Russia and Europe. It has been an official Olympic Games sport since 1920.

Professional hockey is probably the best-known form of the sport and includes teams from both Canada and the United States in the same league. The National Hockey League, founded in 1917, is hockey's major league. Other professional leagues include the American Hockey League, the Central Professional Hockey League and the Western Hockey League.

The National Hockey League is divided into two divisions. In one, the teams include the Boston Bruins, Chicago Black Hawks, Detroit Red Wings, Montreal Canadiens, New York Rangers and Toronto Maple Leafs. In the other, there are the Los Angeles Kings, Minnesota North Stars, Philadelphia Flyers, Pittsburgh Penguins, St. Louis Blues and San Francisco-Oakland Seals. Each team plays a 74-game schedule each winter. The Stanley Cup, presented originally by Lord Stanley, has been awarded each year since 1926 to the National Hockey League play-off winner.

There are many amateur leagues in both countries. Hockey is also a college and high school sport. There are pee-wee, midget and junior leagues for youngsters eight years old and up, too.

This book, in its small way, is intended to help the novice understand the game of ice hockey. It is by no means complete, and each player, spectator, or television viewer is advised to read the rules printed in the back of the book.

The editor wishes to express sincere appreciation to the National Hockey League, especially Don V. Ruck, its Director of Public Relations, for its ever-available help in making this book possible.

ROBERT SCHARFF

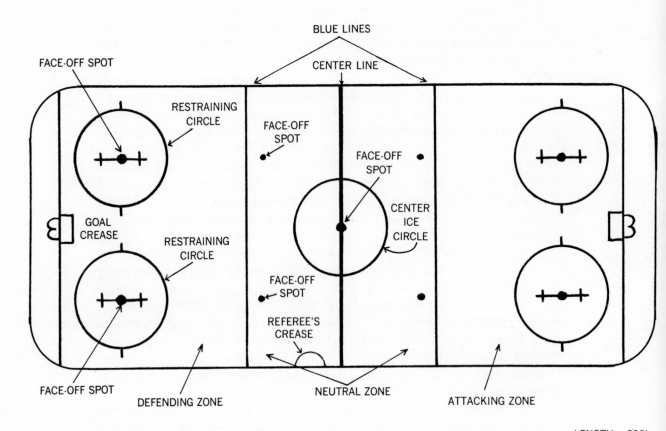

BLUE LINES

CENTER LINE

FACE-OFF SPOT

RESTRAINING CIRCLE

FACE-OFF SPOT

FACE-OFF SPOT

CENTER ICE CIRCLE

GOAL CREASE

RESTRAINING CIRCLE

FACE-OFF SPOT

REFEREE'S CREASE

FACE-OFF SPOT

DEFENDING ZONE

NEUTRAL ZONE

ATTACKING ZONE

LENGTH = 200'

WIDTH = 85'

THE RINK

Hockey's ice surface, or *rink,* is a round-cornered rectangle that is 200 feet long and 85 feet wide (except for some smaller arenas which cannot devote that much space to the game). The rink is surrounded by a wooden wall or fence, known as the *boards,* which is three and a half to four feet high. Tempered plate glass or wire screens generally extend above the boards around the rink to protect the spectators from being hit by the puck.

A two-inch, red goal line, drawn across the width of the ice, is located ten feet from each end of the rink. A six-foot-wide and four-foot-high cage-like goal is centered within each goal line. Two-inch red lines also bound the small area in front of each goal. This area, called the *goal crease,* is eight feet wide and extends four feet from the goal line.

The ice surface between the two goal lines is divided into three portions by 12-inch-wide *blue lines.* They are located parallel to, and 60 feet from, the goal lines. The portion of the ice surface in which the goal is situated is called the *defending zone* of the team defending that goal; the central portion is known as the *neutral zone* (center ice); and the portion farthest from the defended goal as the *attacking zone.* A 12-inch-wide red line, or *center line,* bisects the neutral zone and thus divides the ice surface in half.

The main purposes of these lines are to keep the players on the move, to eliminate permanent stationing of attacking players around an opposing goal, and to give the officials a basis to determine infractions.

In addition to the lines, there are five large circles and four large "dots" on the playing surface. These are used for face-offs, the hockey equivalent to a jump ball in basketball.

The center ice circle is used for face-offs to start play at the opening of each period and after a goal is scored. The two circles inside each blue line are used for face-offs after a penalty or infraction. All circles are 30 feet in diameter and only the two players facing off are permitted within the circles.

The four 12-inch-diameter "dots," inside the neutral zone, are called "face-off spots" and indicate the point of the face-off following a stoppage of play for an offside play or other rule infraction (see Infractions).

Immediately alongside the ice, in the neutral zone, are the players' benches. There are separate door (gate) openings leading from each bench to the ice. Also alongside the ice in the neutral zone are the penalty boxes, or benches, where penalized players must sit out their sentences. There are, of course, separate penalty boxes for each team. On the ice, immediately in front of the penalty timekeeper's seat, there is a red semi-circle of 10-foot radius and two inches in width which is known as the *referee's crease.* When the referee is in this area, during a discussion, players are not permitted to enter it.

Behind each goal, electric lights are set up for the use of the goal judges. A red light signifies the scoring of a goal. Where an automatic light system is employed, a green light signifies the end of a period or a game. A goal cannot be scored when a green light is showing. A buzzer, gong or other suitable sound device is also used to signal the end of a period or a game.

At a rink, there is usually some form of electrical clock for the purpose of keeping the spectators, players and game officials accurately informed of all time elements at all stages of the game, including the time remaining to be played in any period and the time remaining to be served in penalties.

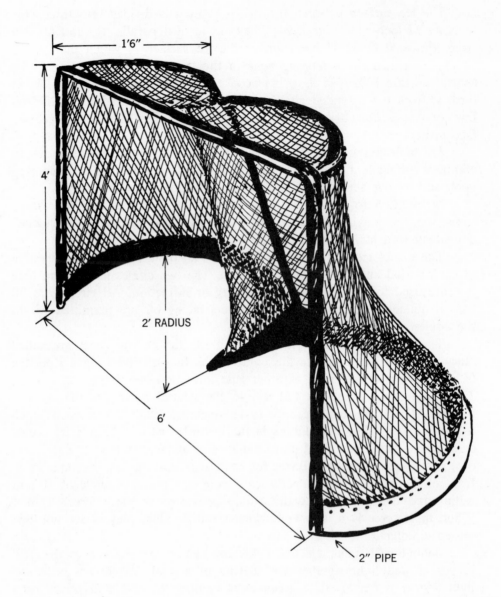

1'6"

4'

2' RADIUS

6'

2" PIPE

The goal net, or cage, is curved in back from one to three feet deep. The sides and back are covered with a white twine netting. The goal is painted red with the exception of the white base at the rear. It is anchored to the ice with pins that extend up through the ice into the pipe-like goal posts. The cage is designed so that pucks entering it will stay in, though occasionally a shot will rebound off a back post and carom out.

THE GAME

The game is of 60 minutes' duration and is divided into three 20-minute periods. (Only actual playing time is counted.) There is a 15-minute intermission. Goals are changed after each period.

The object of the game is to shoot the puck (a hard rubber disk) across the opponent's goal line into the net with a hockey stick. The team scoring the most goals is adjudged the winner, but if the game ends in a tie, special arrangements are made. This depends on the individual league's rules. Some declare a tie game; others play until one team scores.

In league competition, the standing of the teams is determined on a point basis. A team receives two points for each win and one point for a tie. Individual scores are carefully recorded, too, and the competition is often spirited in the race for scoring honors. A player gets one point for each goal he scores and one point for every assist he receives for helping a teammate score.

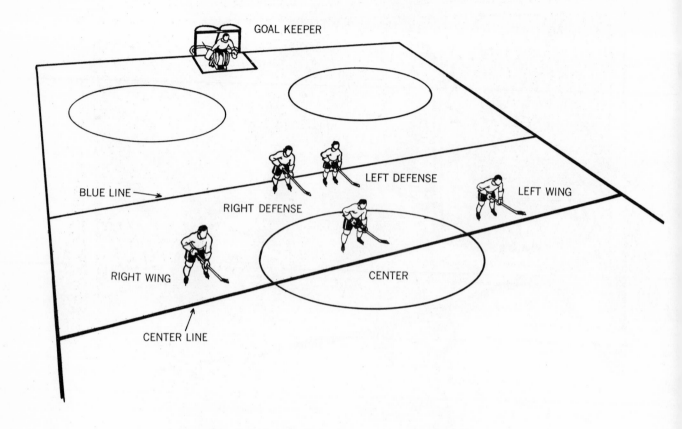

GOAL KEEPER

LEFT DEFENSE

BLUE LINE →

RIGHT DEFENSE

LEFT WING

RIGHT WING

CENTER

CENTER LINE

THE HOCKEY TEAM

A hockey team consists of six players. By positions, they are called the left wing, center, right wing, left defense, right defense, and goalkeeper.

The wingers and center are called forwards and play together on a *line*. There is frequent platooning, but, in general, the same three forwards always play together and the same two defensemen play together. The forwards usually stay on the ice from one to two minutes during a particular time or shift. The defensemen remain in action for longer periods of time, usually three to four minutes. The goalie is the only player who goes the entire 60 minutes of a game.

Here is what each position does:

GOALKEEPER

Goaltender is a breed apart. He must have sharp eyes, quick hands and audacity to stop the 100-mile-per-hour shots by players skating 35 miles per hour. He is the court of last appeal, as it is his responsibility to keep the puck from entering the goal. He can stop the puck in any manner —using his stick, glove or body. He very seldom ever leaves the vicinity of the goalkeeper's crease.

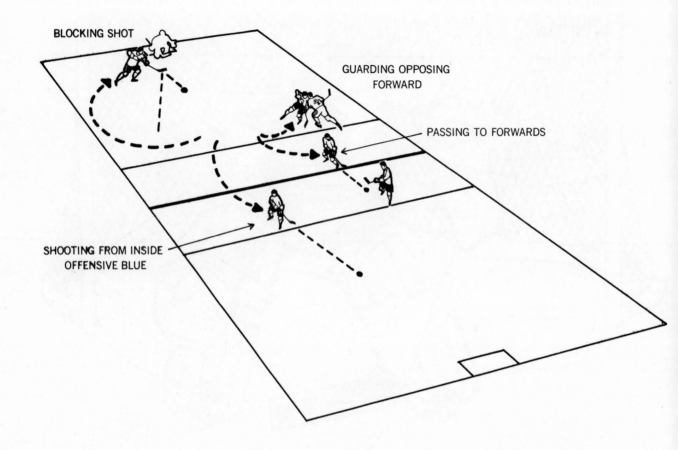

BLOCKING SHOT

GUARDING OPPOSING FORWARD

PASSING TO FORWARDS

SHOOTING FROM INSIDE OFFENSIVE BLUE

DEFENSEMEN

It is their duty to keep the opposition from getting a close shot on the goal. They block shots, clear the puck from in front of the net and guard opposing forwards. Offensively, they pass the puck to the forwards and follow the play to act as a rear guard. The defensemen must also know how to shoot from just inside the attacking blue line (or from what is called the *points*).

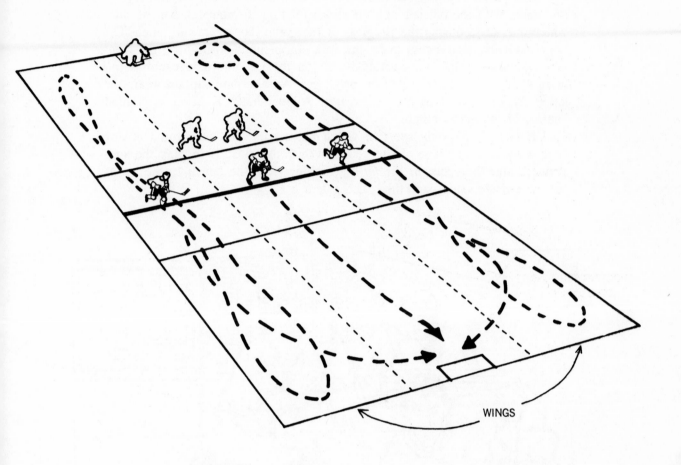

WINGS

FORWARDS

They are the real offensive punch of the team. With the possible exception of facing-off (a special assignment usually given to the center), the forwards must be able to do the same things. For their areas of play, imagine the ice surface divided lengthwise into three equal lanes. The wings are responsible for most of the hockey played in the outside lanes. They stay primarily in their lanes and patrol up and down, moving out only for good reasons. They must be the fastest skaters and the best shots on the team. While the left wings usually are left-handed shooters and the right wings right-handed, there are exceptions.

Generally a team has three lines (nine forwards), four defensemen and a goalie. Most professional teams carry 16 players, plus two goalkeepers. Each player must wear an identifying number at least 10 inches high on the back of his sweater.

One player is appointed team captain, and he alone has the privilege of discussing with the officials any questions relating to interpretation of rules which may arise during the progress of the game. He wears the letter "C," approximately three inches in height, in a conspicuous position on the front of his sweater. When the captain is not on the ice, alternate captains (no more than three) are accorded his privileges. An alternate captain wears the letter "A" on the front of his sweater. A goaltender is never appointed captain or alternate captain.

Hockey is the only sport in which players may be substituted at any time without a stoppage of the action. When the puck is in play the substitutes enter the game *on the fly* by jumping from the bench to the ice as the other players approach the bench gate.

EQUIPMENT

All hockey players wear ice skates, knee-length pants, long stockings, a sweater and heavy protective pads. In addition, sticks and pucks are needed to play the game.

STICKS

Hockey sticks are made of wood (usually white ash or rock elm) and cannot exceed 55 inches from heel to end of shaft. Blade limits are 12½ inches by three inches. The sticks weigh from 17 to 24 ounces. They are curved in the blade to suit a right- or left-handed shooter.

A goalkeeper's stick is wider on the lower shaft and blade than a regular player's stick. The width of this blade may not exceed three and a half inches, except at the heel, where it can be an extra inch wide. This extra width gives the goalie a better surface to deflect a shot.

All sticks are covered with black tape on the blade to conceal the puck, making it harder for opponents to see a shot coming off a stick. Each player planes his stick to his particular desire. A player uses two to four dozen sticks a season.

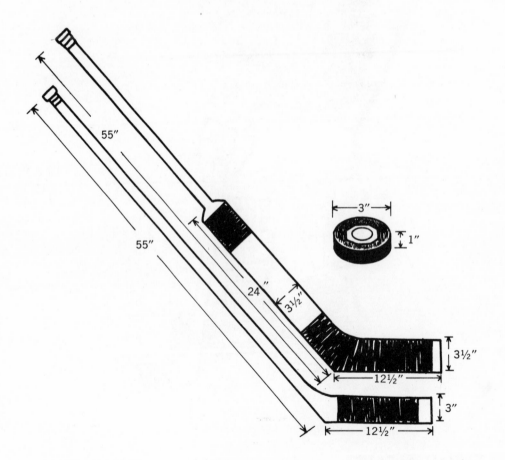

PUCKS

The puck is made of vulcanized rubber, three inches in diameter and one inch thick, and weighs between five and a half and six ounces. Pucks are frozen for several hours before a game to eliminate bouncing. Between 12 and 15 pucks are used during an average game.

SKATES

Only hockey skates can be used in a game. (Speed or figure skates are prohibited.) In addition, all skates worn by players (but not the goalie) and by the officials must be equipped with safety heel tips.

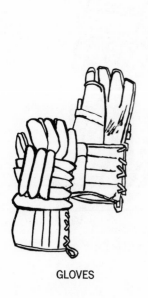

GLOVES

BODY PADDING

SHIN PADS

PROTECTIVE EQUIPMENT

Each player wears the following protective gear:

Gloves—individually padded thumbs and fingers. Fiber gauntlet covers wrists and forearms.

Elbow Pads—made of leather covered with felt or foam rubber.

Shoulder Pads—similar to those used in football

Shin Pads—made of fiber or plastic with a felt knee pad on top.

In addition, some players wear head-gear or helmets, kidney and thigh pads. All protective equipment except gloves and head-gear must be worn under the uniform (the stockings, pants and sweaters). Much of this protective equipment is cushioned with foam rubber.

17

MASK

GLOVES

KNEE, SHIN PADS

GOALKEEPER'S EQUIPMENT

The goalie usually wears special skates. The flat, low blade gives him better balance and is constructed to stop pucks from passing between the blade and the shoe. He wears overstuffed, ribbed, leg pads that are ten inches wide and extend from the ankles to above the knees. Under his sweater, or jersey, he wears a heavy felt chest protector which also covers the shoulders, stomach, abdomen and arms. Goalkeepers' gloves are of a different design than those of the other players. The glove for the catching hand resembles a first baseman's mitt with a long cuff, while the one worn on the stick hand is well padded. Some goalies wear masks for face protection. A goalkeeper's equipment weighs about 40 pounds, compared to 20 pounds for each of the other players.

OFFICIALS

There are eight officials in hockey—the referee, two linesmen, two goal judges, a penalty timekeeper, the official scorer, and a game timekeeper.

RED ARM BAND

THE REFEREE

The *referee* has full control of a hockey game. While he receives assistance from the linesmen and goal judges, the final decision on everything, from the time a game will start to whether or not a goal beat the buzzer, rests with the referee. He is the only official with power to administer a penalty that will put a man off the ice. However, he does not call infractions of icing, offside and offside passes.

Although the referee and linesmen are clad in identical uniforms, the referee can be distinguished by a red arm band. The referee can only be replaced if an illness or accident makes it impossible for him to continue. Then he appoints one of the linesmen to take his place.

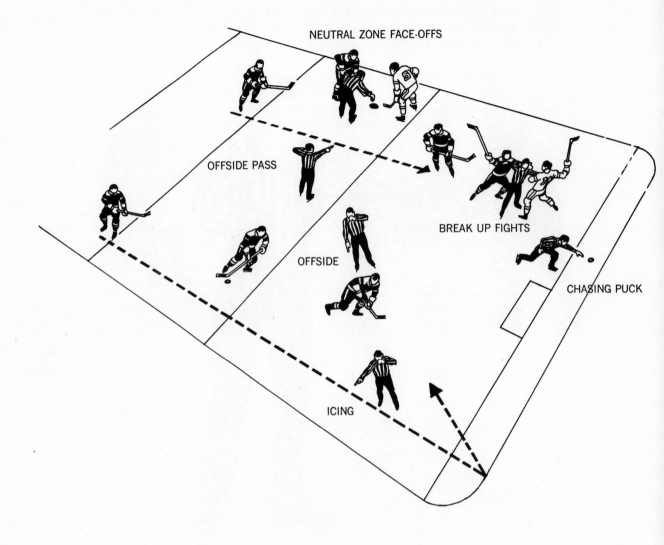

NEUTRAL ZONE FACE-OFFS

OFFSIDE PASS

OFFSIDE

BREAK UP FIGHTS

CHASING PUCK

ICING

THE LINESMEN

The *linesmen* call the infractions of icing, offside, and offside passes. They chase the puck after stoppage of play and drop the puck for face-offs in the neutral zone. They cannot call penalties but can report these infractions to the referee. The referee may call upon a linesman to give his version of an incident that may take place during a game. And it is their unenviable job to break up fights while the referee assesses the penalties.

In many amateur leagues, there is only one linesman.

THE GOAL JUDGES

The *goal judges* are seated in a screened area, outside the playing surface, behind each goal. It is their job to determine whether or not the puck has crossed the goal line. (The referee, of course, has the final decision on the legality of goals.) If it has, a red light in front of the goal judge's area is turned on to signify a score.

THE PENALTY TIMEKEEPER

The *penalty timekeeper* checks the time served by penalized players and keeps an accurate account of the time penalties are imposed and elapsed.

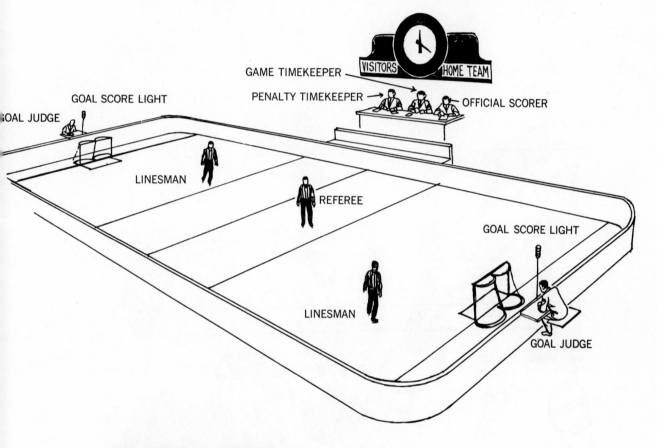

THE OFFICIAL SCORER

The *official scorer* keeps the official score sheet to record goals scored, the scorers, players to whom assists have been credited, goalkeepers' saves and the time of penalties. The referee reports to the official scorer the name or number of the goal scorer, but the official scorer credits the assists.

THE GAME TIMEKEEPER

The *game timekeeper* operates the master clock which tells how much time has elapsed in each period, and he is responsible for the buzzer, gong, or other sound device which signals the end of a period.

HOCKEY ACTION

As the game is about to start, both teams line up in position on the ice for the opening face-off. The center is at the center spot in the neutral zone, flanked by his left and right wings. The wings are about midway between the edge of the restraining circle and the boards and a few feet on their own side of the center line. The two defensemen station themselves near their own blue line, about ten feet apart. The goalkeeper stands between the goalposts just inside his crease line. The referee is at center ice with the puck, facing the game timekeeper, while the linesmen stand at the side boards facing each other, but on opposite blue lines.

The game is actually started by a face-off at the center spot. The two opposing centers stand squarely facing their opponent's end of the rink about one stick length apart, one foot on either side of the line through the

face-off spot and with full blade of the stick flat on the ice. When the puck, dropped by the referee, strikes the ice, the players facing off play it with their sticks. No other player may enter the restraining circle until this occurs.

Players can move the puck down the ice with their sticks, skates, or bodies. They skate swiftly, weaving, dodging, zig-zagging, as they drive, or rush, toward the opponent's goal. Defending players try to get the puck away from the attackers by blocking or checking them with either their bodies or their sticks, or by intercepting the puck. It is not necessary to shoot the puck into the netting behind the goalie to score. If the entire puck crosses the goal line inside the posts, even if it is in the possession of the goalkeeper, it is a goal:

1. Unless an attacking player kicks the puck, or throws the puck, or otherwise deliberately directs the puck into the goal by any means other than the stick.

2. Unless an attacking player is in the goal crease and is in no way held in by a defender while a teammate "scores."

It is within the rules for an attacking player to carry the puck into the goal crease area and still score. It is also within the rules for an attacking side to score a goal by having a shot deflect off a teammate, as long as the teammate does not intentionally steer the deflection into the goal with his hand or skate.

If the same shot deflects into the goal off a defender, or if a defender inadvertently directs the puck over the goal line, it is a goal. In such a case, the attacking player who last played the puck, in the referee's opinion, is awarded the goal. No assists are given.

While a goal does not count if it is kicked in by an attacker, if that same attacker kicks it in off a defender other than the goalkeeper, it does count. In this case, the kicker is credited with the goal. On the other hand, if a shot is deflected in off a teammate, the teammate gets credit for the goal and the shooter gets an assist.

No more than two assists can be credited on any goal, and those assists go to the two players who handle the puck immediately preceding the goal.

HOCKEY TECHNIQUES

Hockey combines the skills of many sports: the ruggedness of a football player; the finesse of a baseball player; the strength of a weight lifter; the coordination of a golfer; and the endurance of a distance runner or a channel swimmer. But, success in playing hockey is first, last and always based upon the mastery of the basic fundamentals of skating, stick-handling, passing, shooting and checking. For the spectator to fully appreciate the sport, he should know about the hockey techniques involved in these skills.

SKATING

In hockey everything begins with skating. It is what the player does most. It is the foundation on which the other fundamentals are built. National Hockey League scouts intimate that players are prevented from reaching the "big league" more by a lack of skating skill than anything else.

In analyzing hockey skating (pleasure, speed and figure skating are completely different propositions), most experts agree that there are several types of skating techniques, but these can be broken down into the following three categories:

FREE SKATING. This is the straightaway skating that a player does on open ice, either with or without the puck.

BACKWARD SKATING. This type of skating is employed when checking a puck-carrier, covering an opponent, or maneuvering to get free during a power play.

AGILITY SKATING. This is the sum of all the other skating skills that the player needs for checking, puck-carrying, stopping quickly, cutting sharply, breaking away, changing pace, etc.

Most professional players are from Canada and have been skating since they learned to walk. These young players, for the most part, have never had to concentrate on learning the fundamentals of hockey skating, for almost as soon as they don their first pair of skates, they start to use a hockey stick. Witnessing a professional game will bear out this fact.

25

STICKHANDLING

Stickhandling is the carrying of the puck along the ice with the stick. This technique is one of the two ways a player can get the puck out of his end, down the ice, and into the scoring zone. The other method is by passing the puck, but of the two, stickhandling is much more thrilling to the spectator.

In stickhandling, the player is, in a sense, passing the puck to himself. He advances the puck from side to side with soft sweeps, varying in width from three to four inches to as wide as he can reach. For best control, the puck is nursed midway on the blade.

Hockey is really a game of moves and countermoves. This is especially true when the player stickhandles his way down ice. Actually, the puck-carrier always tries to force his opponent to commit himself first. Then he will base his countermove on the opponent's definite move. Sometimes the smart player will fake, or "deke," his opponent into a commitment before applying the countermove.

PASSING

Passing the puck between teammates is the real basis of hockey team play. As the game is played today, the passing has replaced stickhandling to some degree. The pass permits a more wide-open type of play and enables the player to bypass checkers with a pass to a teammate in situations that once would have required him to stickhandle expertly to get out of trouble. Passing is also the quickest way to get the puck in the scoring zone since the puck-carrier usually tries to pass to the man in front of him. In former days, the popular way of getting into the attacking zone was to stickhandle in as far as possible and then pass off. Today's trend is to shoot the puck over the attacking blue-line and against the boards. Then follow it up, gain possession and pass the puck around until a player gets a clear shot at the goal.

It often amazes the first-time watcher of hockey how accurately a good player can spot and pass to his teammate. This is because he has developed what is called *split vision*—the ability to look straight ahead and yet see players on either side.

There are several types of passes used in hockey:

SWEEP PASS. In making a sweep pass, the player moves the puck in the desired direction with a smooth, sweeping motion, avoiding any quick, jerky action. On the follow-through, the blade of the stick will move along on the ice so that the pass will not be lifted. (Follow-through is the path that the stick follows in the direction of the puck after a pass or shot has been made.) This pass is employed when deception is not an important factor or when the puck-carrier has plenty of time to set up the pass.

SNAP PASS. This pass is used mainly when there is little time in which to make the pass or if the puck-carrier wants to make a quick, unexpected pass in the midst of a stickhandling pattern. To make this type of pass the puck is sent on its way by a quick snap of the wrists. There is no sweep motion whatsoever.

FLIP PASS. A flip pass is made from the toe of the stickblade and is made with a quick flip of the wrist. It is used when the puck-carrier desires to raise the puck over an opponent's stick, a player on the ice or, perhaps, between the defense, or from out of a scramble. When the puck is to cover some distance off the ice, the *lift pass* is employed. The technique used is the same as for a sweep pass except the blade of the stick is lifted off the ice during the follow-through.

SLAP PASS. This is a quick pass that is used when the puck comes to a player in the midst of a scramble or when the man receiving a pass wishes to get the puck to a teammate without first stopping it. It is made by bringing the stick back a short distance, then quickly forward and slapping the puck in the desired direction.

All these passing techniques can be made forward, lateral, backward, or diagonal, and can be made either backhand or forehand.

ENEMY GOAL

DROP PASS. With a drop pass, the puck-carrier leaves the puck behind to be picked up by a trailing teammate. In making this pass, the puck-carrier carries the puck forward, then quickly moves his stickblade ahead of the puck and gives it a sharp, backward, choppy slap, so that the forward progress of the puck is stopped dead.

SHOOTING

Since scoring a goal is the object of the game, there can be little doubt of the importance of shooting. The shooter generally aims at the four vulnerable corners—upper left and right, and lower left and right—of the cage since these are the hardest for a goalie to defend. The following, which can be either forehand or backhand, are basic shots that are most commonly seen in a hockey game:

SWEEP SHOT. This shot, often called the *power shot,* is named be-cause it is performed with a smooth, sweeping action of the stick. The stick and full weight of the body follow through into the shot, with arms, wrists and back all contributing to produce power. It can be shot as an "ice hugger" or lifted, by snapping the wrists, to the upper portion of the cage.

SNAP SHOT. A snap shot, which is often called a *wrist shot,* is decep-tive and effective because it is done quickly and with a tremendous wrist snap. It is used, for example, after taking a pass in front of the goal or after a fake (deke) has drawn the goalie out of position.

SLAP SHOT. This shot has tremendous power and is a surprise shot. While it lacks the accuracy of the sweep shot, it is highly effective because its blinding speed and electrifying suddenness deny the goaltender any chance to set himself. The slap shot is made by bringing the stick back, then quickly forward and slapping the puck ahead. It can be accomplished by stopping the puck first, then teeing off on it; or the slap may be made at a soft pass-out or rebound without stopping the puck.

FLIP SHOT. The flip shot is a technique used to hit the upper corners of the net from close in or to lift the puck over a sprawling goalkeeper. The lift is given by tilting the blade so that only its bottom edge contacts the puck, and the shot is made in the same manner as a flip pass.

CHECKING

Checking is the defensive move of blocking a player out of a play or regaining possession of the puck by "stealing" it from the attacker's stick. While good checking technique is a requirement for forwards and defensemen alike, the latter must be specialists in the art.

There are three basic methods of stick checking: the *sweep check,* the *hook check,* and the *poke check.* In the latter, the puck is dislodged from the puck-carrier by a quick stabbing or jabbing at it with the blade of the stick, while the hook check is accomplished by the snaking or whipping of the stick as flat as possible on the ice and trapping the puck inside the hook so formed. A sweep check is made by sweeping the stick very quickly in a semicircle towards the oncoming puck-carrier, with as much of the stick flat on the ice as possible in order to dislodge the puck from the attacker's stick. While this check covers a lot of ice surface and is difficult for the puck-carrier to avoid, possession is seldom gained because the puck is usually knocked some distance away.

To block the progress of an opponent, a *bodycheck* is employed. It is permitted only with the torso (shoulder to hip—never the leg) and can be preceded by no more than two steps, or strides, toward the puck-carrier. The most effective and stunning bodycheck is made by thrusting the shoulder into the onrushing player's chest. In order to assure a solid check, the defending player must concentrate completely on the body of the puck-carrier (disregarding the puck altogether) and step into him as he comes within bodychecking range. The best time to bodycheck is when the puck-carrier is occupied with other considerations—namely, when starting a pass or receiving a pass.

GOALTENDING

The goalkeeper is the most important player on the hockey team. The mistakes of any of the other players can usually be compensated for, but when the goalie has a "bad" day the results are generally disastrous.

When the puck is at the opposite end of the ice, the goalie may relax to some extent. He may spend better than half the game under fire in his own end; therefore he must learn to save himself for the maximum efforts that he will surely be called upon to make later in the game. When the puck reaches center ice, or is in the defensive zone, he adopts the "ready" position. That is, the feet are wide enough apart to keep the pads closed. The knees are bent just enough to allow him to move quickly either to the left or right. He bends forward at the waist to bring his eyes closer to ice level, and to allow the stick to be kept flat on the ice in front of his skates. The stick is held by one hand at the botton of the narrow part of the shaft, while the free, or catching, hand is held beside the leg. From this stance, the goalie moves in a small arc from side to side of the net, keeping his body at all times centered on the puck.

The goaltender employs his stick to stop as many shots along the ice as it can reach. His free hand is used to catch all pucks off the ice to the strong side, to trap high shots taken on the body and to smother loose pucks on the ice when he has to go down. High shots to the weak side may be deflected by the back of the stick hand.

There are many tricks and moves that the goalie must make in stopping the puck when it is shot in different ways at different parts of the goal area. For example, he may do the "splits" to make a "save" (or stop) on a low shot well to his side. (In making this maneuver, as its name implies, the goaltender does the splits exactly as done by a dancer.) He may make saves by a kicking motion, by using his stick or by sprawling across the cage. One of his best weapons is to cut down the shooting angle, or opening, and make it more difficult for the shooter to score. To do this, the goalie moves out to the front line of the goal crease, or even further, and directly at the puck's position so that both corners of the net are virtually closed off.

INFRACTIONS

Three main rules—icing, offsides, and offside passes—cover the majority of infractions in hockey. They are "spectator designed" as they force play-making and teamwork, discourage stalling and maintain speed. The three infractions are governed by the blue lines and center red line, and each calls for a face-off.

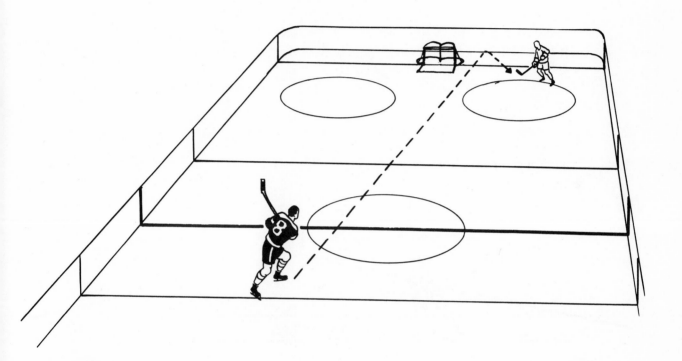

ICING THE PUCK

Icing the puck occurs when a player shoots the puck up the ice from his side of the red center line and across the opposing team's goal line (not into the goal, of course), and the puck is first touched by an opposing player. Play is stopped and the puck is then brought back for a face-off in the circle deep in the zone of the offending team.

There are four conditions when icing is not called:

1. When a team is shorthanded as a result of a penalty, it cannot be called for icing. (Shorthanded means that the team is below the numerical strength of its opponents.)

2. When a defending opponent, in the judgment of the linesman could have played the puck before it crossed his own goal line, there is no icing.

3. If the puck cuts across part of the goal crease, no icing will be called.

4. When a member of the team which ices the puck touches it before the defending opponent, no icing is called and play continues.

OFFSIDES

An *offside* occurs when any member of the attacking team crosses the defending team's "blue line" ahead of the puck. For violation of this rule, the play is stopped, and the puck is faced-off in the neutral zone at the point from which the pass was made, or at the attacking zone of the offending team if the pass was made within five feet of the line.

The position of the player's skates and not that of his stick is the determining factor in all instances in deciding an "offside." That is, a player is "onside" when *either* of his skates are in contact with or on his own side of the blue line at the instant the puck completely crosses the outer edge of that line regardless of the position of his stick. Should the skates of the player propelling the puck cross the line ahead of the puck, it is considered an "offside."

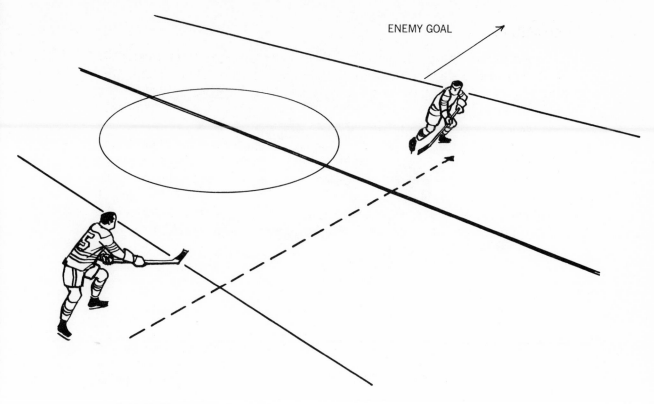

ENEMY GOAL

OFFSIDE PASS

An "offside pass" occurs and produces an immediate stoppage of play when a player passes or deflects the puck from the defending zone to a team-mate beyond the center red-line *unless* the pass receiver was himself in the defending zone at the time the puck crossed the defending blue-line.

The position of the puck (not the player's skates) is the determining factor in deciding from which zone the pass was made.

PUCK OUT-OF-BOUNDS OR UNPLAYABLE

When the puck goes outside the playing area at either end, or either side of the rink or strikes any obstacle above the playing surface other than the boards, glass or wire, it is faced-off from where it was shot or deflected.

If the puck becomes lodged in the netting on the outside of either goal making it unplayable, or when it is "frozen" between opposing players in-tentionally or otherwise, the referee stops play, and the puck is faced-off at either of the adjacent face-off spots. If the referee believes that the stop-page was caused by a player of the attacking team, he can conduct the face-off in the neutral zone.

Should a scramble take place, or if a player accidentally falls on the puck, and the puck is out of sight of the referee, he immediately blows his whistle and stops the play. The puck then is faced-off at the point where the play was stopped.

PENALTIES

Penalties play a more important role in the outcome of a hockey game than in any other sport. Usually several times during the game each team will be forced to play shorthanded when one or more of its players is sent to the penalty box. At no time, however, is a team made to play more than two men below full strength. Should a third penalty be called, it is delayed until the first expires. Nevertheless, the third player penalized must at once proceed to the penalty box but may be replaced by a substitute until such time as the penalty time of the guilty man commences.

TEAM WITH THE ADVANTAGE

PENALIZED TEAM "PENALTY KILLERS"

When a team is penalized, the entire strategy of the game changes on both sides. The penalized team puts its best defensive players—called *penalty killers*—on the ice. The team with the advantage plays its best offensive players, known as the *power play unit*.

There are six classifications: 1) minor penalties; 2) bench minor penalties; 3) major penalties; 4) misconduct penalties; 5) match penalties; and 6) penalty shot.

MINOR PENALTIES

A minor penalty calls for a player, except the goalkeeper, to be ruled off the ice for two minutes during which time no substitute is permitted.

BENCH MINOR PENALTIES

A bench minor penalty involves the removal, for two minutes, of one player of the team against which the penalty is awarded. Any player of the team may be designated, by the manager or coach, to serve the penalty, but the selected man takes his seat in the penalty box and serves the penalty as if it were a minor penalty imposed upon him.

If, while a team is shorthanded by one or more minor or bench minor penalties, the opposing team scores, the *first* of such penalties is automatically terminated. There is no exception. If a shorthanded team, for instance, incurs a penalty shot against it, and the penalty shot succeeds, a player is released from the penalty box.

MAJOR PENALTY

For the first *major penalty* in a game, the offender, except the goaltender, is ruled off the ice for five minutes, during which time no substitute for him is permitted. If the second major penalty occurs in the same game to the same player, he is banished to the penalty box for 15 minutes, but a substitute is permitted after five minutes have elapsed. The third major penalty to the same player in the same game means his expulsion from the remainder of the contest, but a substitute is permitted to replace the man so suspended after five minutes have elapsed. In professional hockey, a fine may also accompany a major penalty.

When coincident major penalties are imposed against an equal number of players of each team, the penalized players must take their seats in the penalty boxes, and they are not allowed to leave until the first stoppage of play following the expiry of their respective penalties. Immediate substitutions may be made for the players so penalized and neither team is considered shorthanded.

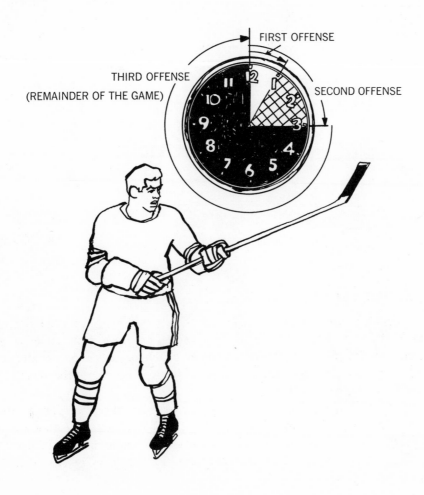

43

MISCONDUCT PENALTIES

A *misconduct penalty* is a ten-minute penalty, generally called against a player who becomes abusive in language or gesture. It puts him out for ten minutes but does not leave his team shorthanded. In professional hockey, it is also accompanied by an automatic fine against the offender.

When a player receives a minor penalty and a misconduct penalty at the same time, the penalized team immediately puts a substitute player in the penalty box, and he serves the minor penalty as if imposed upon him. In the case of both a major penalty and misconduct one, the penalized team sends a substitute player to the penalty box before the major penalty expires since no replacement for a penalized player may enter the game except from the penalty bench.

A *game misconduct* penalty involves the suspension of a player for the balance of the game, but a substitute is permitted to replace him immediately. In professional hockey, there is an automatic fine against the offender.

(1) ATTEMPT TO INJURE

(2) DELIBERATE INJURY

MATCH PENALTIES

A *match penalty* means immediate ejection of the guilty player for the balance of the game. It is levied for (1) deliberate *attempt to injure,* wherein a substitute can be used after five minutes or (2) deliberate *injury* to an opponent, calling for ten minutes without replacement. In professional hockey, there is usually further suspension and fine to the offender of a match penalty.

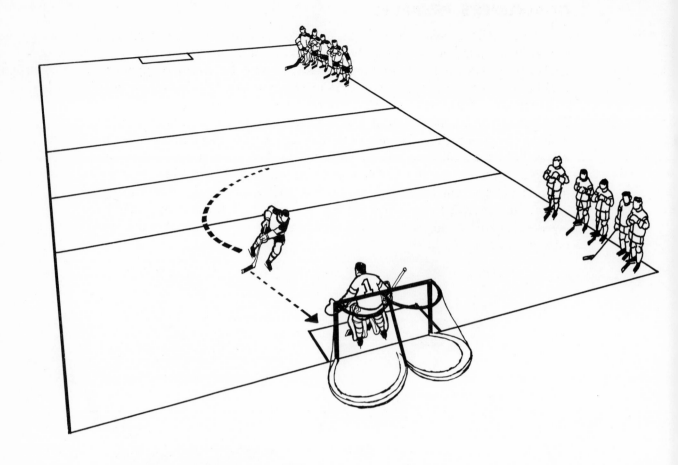

PENALTY SHOT

The *penalty shot* gives a player a clear shot at the goal with only the goalie to defend. It is awarded a player who is illegally impeded from behind when in possession of the puck and with no opponent between him and the opponent's goal, except the goalkeeper.

The player designated by the referee to take the penalty shot may carry the puck in from any part of the neutral zone or his own defending zone, but once the puck has crossed the attacking blue line it must be kept in motion towards the opponent's goal line, and once it is shot, the play is considered complete. (No goal can be scored on a rebound of any kind, and any time the puck crosses the goal line the shot is considered completed.) The goalie must remain in his goal crease until the puck has crossed the adjacent blue line. While the penalty shot is being taken, players of both sides must withdraw to the sides of the rink and beyond the center red line. The offending team does not play shorthanded after the penalty shot, whether successful or not.

If a goal is scored from a penalty shot the puck is faced-off at center ice in the usual way. If a goal is not scored the puck is faced-off at either of the end face-off spots in the zone in which the penalty shot was tried.

GOALKEEPER'S PENALTIES

If a goalie is assessed a minor or major penalty, his time is always served by a teammate designated by the manager or coach. In the case of a goalkeeper's incurring a misconduct penalty, it must be served by another member of his team (designated by the manager or coach), *who was on the ice* when the offense was committed. Should a goalie incur a game misconduct penalty or a match penalty, his place is taken by a member of his own club, or by a substitute goaltender if one is available, and this player is allowed to put on all the goalie's equipment. In the case of a match penalty, any time in the penalty box covered under the rules will be served by another member of the team on the ice at the time of the offense. In professional hockey, the goalkeeper is subject to fine for major, misconduct and match penalties as well as for leaving the immediate vicinity of his goal crease to take part in a fight.

CALLING OF PENALTIES

When a minor, major or match penalty is committed by a player of the side in possession of the puck, the referee immediately blows his whistle and gives the penalty to the deserving player. The resulting face-off is held at the spot where the play was stopped unless the stoppage occurred in the attacking zone of the player penalized. In such a case, the face-off is made at the nearest face-off spot in the neutral zone.

Should a minor, major or match penalty be called on a player of the team *not* in possession of the puck, the referee signifies the calling of a penalty by pointing to the offending player. On completion of the play by the team in possession, he blows his whistle and gives the penalty to the deserving player. ("Completion of the play by the team in possession" in this rule simply means that the puck must have come into complete possession and control of an opposing player or has been "frozen." This does not mean a rebound off the goalie or any accidental contact with the body or equipment of an opposing player.) If the penalty to be imposed is a minor one, and a goal is scored on the play *by the nonoffending* side, the penalty is nullified. However, in the case of a major or match penalty, it is imposed in the normal manner regardless of whether a goal is scored or not.

FOULS

The phrase "never a dull moment" may well have been coined at a hockey game by a spectator who needed words to describe the furious action of this speed-burning sport. This is true because hockey is competitive excitement maintained at a continuous breakneck pace. But, because of the great speed at which hockey is played, it is essential that the officials carefully call all fouls and mete out the necessary penalties so the game does not get "out-of-hand" and serious injuries do not occur to its participants. Even so, penalties often result in anger between the offender and the offended, producing what the hockey rule book calls an altercation, or fisticuffs. And fights (a better word) between two players and brawls (the best description) where both teams fill the ice for a slugfest are commonplace in a sport where body contact at high speeds tends to make tempers short.

The severity of any foul depends on official interpretation and sometimes on the degree of violence. For example, a player can be "ridden off" along the boards but cannot be slammed into the boards. Often a minor penalty is changed to a major one if a patent injury is caused, but this again is a matter of judgment. Conversely, some fights are adjudged to be roughing, an offender drawing two minutes, or four instead of five. But any player who deliberately injures an opponent, in the opinion of the referee, receives a match penalty. Hockey is a fast, rough, tough sport in which "dirty" play has no place.

DELAYING THE GAME

A bench minor penalty is imposed upon any team that causes unnecessary delays in the game or has too many players on the ice at one time.

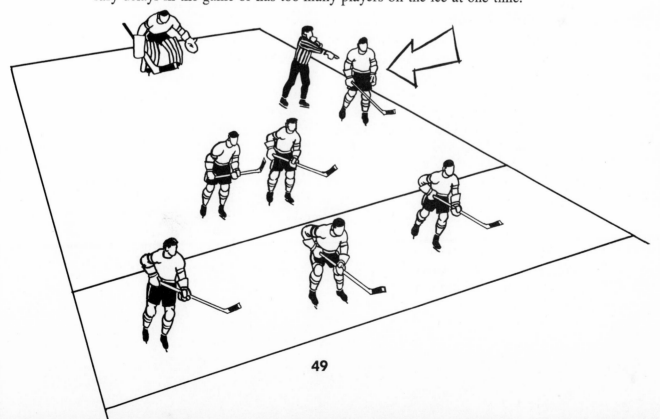

INTERFERENCE

A minor penalty is imposed on a player who interferes with or impedes the progress of an opponent who is *not* in possession of the puck. In interpreting this rule, the referee must make sure which of the players is the one creating the interference. Often it is the action and movement of the attacking player which cause the interference since the defending players are entitled to "stand their ground" or "shadow" the attacking players. Players of the side in possession are not permitted to "run" deliberate interference for the puck carrier.

A minor penalty is assessed on a player on the players' bench or in the penalty box who, by means of his stick or his body, interferes with the movements of the puck or of any opponent on the ice.

A minor penalty is given to a player who, by means of his stick or his body, interferes with or impedes the movements of the goalkeeper by actual physical contact, while he is in his goal crease area (unless the puck is already in that area).

CROSS-CHECKING

A minor or major penalty, at the discretion of the referee, is assigned to a player who cross-checks. This means a check delivered with both hands on the stick and no part of the stick on the ice.

CHARGING

A minor or major penalty is imposed on a player who runs or jumps into or charges an opponent.

A minor or major penalty is inflicted on a player who charges a goalkeeper while the goalie is within his goal crease. If more than two steps or strides are taken, it is considered a charge.

HOLDING

A minor penalty is awarded to a player who holds an opponent with hands or stick, or in any other way.

HOOKING

A minor penalty is given to a player who impedes or seeks to impede the progress of an opponent by "hooking" with his stick. When a player is checking another in such a way that there is only stick-to-stick contact such action is *neither* holding nor hooking.

TRIPPING

A minor penalty is imposed on any player who places his stick, knee, foot, arm, hand or elbow in such a manner that it causes his opponent to trip or fall. When a player, in control of the puck in the attacking zone and having no other opponent to pass than the goaltender, is tripped, a penalty shot is awarded to the nonoffending side.

SLASHING

A minor or major penalty, at the discretion of the referee, is assigned to a player who impedes or seeks to impede the progress of an opponent by "slashing" with his stick. The referee can also call slashing on any player who swings his stick at any opponent (whether in or out of range) without actually striking him or where a player, on the pretext of playing the puck, makes a wild swing at the puck with the object of intimidating an opponent. This rule goes further: Any player who swings his stick at another player in the course of an altercation is subject to a match penalty plus the likelihood of a heavy fine and suspension. This is why hockey players drop their sticks at the start of a fight—so they will not be tempted to use them if the going becomes tough.

HIGH-STICKING

A minor or major penalty may be given for using a high stick against an opponent. Carrying a stick above shoulder level calls for stoppage of play and a face-off at the spot where the offense occurred.

ELBOWING AND KNEEING

A minor or major penalty may be awarded to any player who uses his elbow or knee to check an opponent. A match penalty is imposed on a player who kicks or attempts to kick another.

BOARDING

A minor or major penalty, based upon the degree of violence of the impact with the boards, is imposed on any player who body-checks, cross-checks, elbows, charges or trips an opponent in such a manner that causes that player to crash violently into the boards. However, "rolling" an opponent (if he is the puck-carrier) along the boards where he is endeavoring to go through too small an opening is not boarding. If the opponent is not the puck-carrier, such action will be penalized as boarding, charging, interference, or, if the arms or stick are employed, it will be called holding or hooking.

SPEARING

A minor, major, or even a match penalty may be given to a player who spears or attempts to spear an opponent. (Spearing is stabbing an opponent with the point of the stick blade.)

BUTT ENDING

A minor or major penalty is imposed on a player who hits his opponent with the butt end of his stick, while both hands are on the stick and no part of the stick is on the ice.

FIGHTING

A major, double minor or minor penalty may be handed out to a player who starts a fight. In turn, a minor penalty is awarded to the man who, having been struck, retaliates with a blow or attempted blow. However, the referee is provided very wide latitude in the penalties which he may impose under this rule. This is done intentionally to enable him to differentiate between the obvious degrees of responsibility of the participants either for starting the fighting or persisting in continuing the fighting.

ROUGHING

At the discretion of the referee, a minor penalty may be given to a player whom he deems guilty of unnecessary roughness.

BROKEN STICK

A player whose stick is broken may stay on the ice provided he drops the broken portion. A minor penalty is imposed for failure to abide with this rule.

A player on the ice can only obtain a new stick from his players' bench, while the goalkeeper may receive a replacement stick from a teammate who has obtained it from the players' bench. A minor penalty, plus a misconduct one, is imposed on the player or goalie receiving a stick by any other means.

THROWING A STICK

When a player of the defending side, including the goalie, deliberately throws his stick or any part thereof, at the puck in his defending zone, the referee allows the play to be completed, and if a goal is not scored, a penalty shot is awarded to the nonoffending team.

A major penalty is given to a player who throws his stick or any other object, in any zone, except when such an act has been penalized by the award of a penalty shot. However, when a player discards the broken portion of a stick by tossing it to the side of the ice (and not over the boards) in a way that will not interfere with play or opposing players, no penalty is imposed.

HANDLING PUCK WITH HANDS

If a player (except the goalie) closes his hand on the puck the play is stopped and a minor penalty is imposed on him. He is permitted, however, to stop or "bat" a puck in the air with his open hand. He may also push it along the ice with his hand and the play will not be stopped unless, in the opinion of the referee, he has *deliberately* directed the puck to a teammate. When play is stopped by the referee, the puck is faced-off at the spot where the offense occurred.

A goalkeeper must not deliberately hold the puck in any manner which, in the opinion of the referee, causes an *unnecessary* stoppage of play. This includes deliberately dropping the puck into his pads or onto the goal net. Also, the goalie cannot throw the puck forward towards the opponents' goal. The penalty for such violations is a minor penalty.

FALLING ON PUCK

A minor penalty is imposed on a player other than the goalkeeper who deliberately falls on a puck or gathers it into his body. Defensemen who drop to their knees to block shots are not penalized if the puck is shot under them or becomes lodged in their clothing or equipment, but any use of the hands to make the puck unplayable is illegal.

FACE-OFF VIOLATION

During a face-off no player facing-off should make any physical contact with his opponent's body by means of his own body or by his stick except in the course of playing the puck after the face-off has been completed. For violation of this rule, the referee may impose a minor penalty or penalties on the player(s) whose action(s) caused the physical contact.

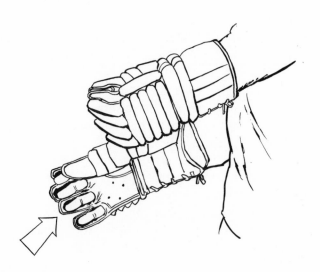

EQUIPMENT VIOLATION

Any player, including the goalie, is subject to a minor penalty for the use of illegal equipment, protective gear, or stick.

OFFICIALS' CODE OF SIGNALS

While all penalties, offenses and the time they occurred are announced over the public address system, referees have different signals for common fouls which are as follows:

INTERFERENCE.   Crossed arms stationary in front of the chest.

CROSS-CHECKING.   A series of forward and backward motions with both fists clenched, extending from the chest.

CHARGING.   Rotating clenched fists around one another in front of the chest.

HOLDING.   Clasping either wrist with the other hand well in front of the chest.

HOOKING.   A series of tugging motions with both arms, as if pulling something toward the stomach.

TRIPPING.   Extending the right leg forward, clear of the ice, and striking it with the right hand below the knee.

SLASHING.   A series of chopping motions with the edge of one hand across the opposite forearm.

ELBOWING.   Tapping either elbow with the opposite hand.

BOARDING.   Pounding the closed fist of one hand into the open palm of the other hand.

MISCONDUCT PENALTY.   Placing of both hands on hips several times and pointing to the penalized player.

DELAYED CALLING OF PENALTY.   Referee repeatedly points with free hand (without whistle) to player to be penalized when play stops.

ICING.   Arms folded across the chest. When the puck is shot or deflected in such a manner as to produce a possible icing of the puck the *rear linesman* will signal to his partner by raising either arm over his head (same as in slow whistle signal). Immediately after the conditions required to establish "icing the puck" have occurred, the *forward linesman* will respond with the same slow whistle signal, and the *rear linesman* will blow his whistle to stop the play and both will give the proper "icing signal."

SLOW WHISTLE.   Either hand, in which the whistle is held, is raised above head. If play returns to neutral zone without stoppage, the hand is drawn down the instant the puck crosses the line.

"WASH-OUT."   Both arms swing laterally across the body with the palms down:

1. When used by the referee it means goal disallowed.
2. When used by the linesmen it means there is no icing or no offside.

SLASHING

ELBOWING

HOLDING

CHARGING

BOARDING

CROSS-CHECKING

INTERFERENCE

ICING

MISCONDUCT PENALTY

WASHOUT

HOOKING

TRIPPING

SLOW WHISTLE

DELAYED CALLING OF PENALTY

HOCKEY TERMS

BACK CHECK. An attempt by forwards, on their way back to their defensive zone, to regain the puck from the opposition.

BACKHAND. A shot or pass taken on the left side of a right-handed player or the right side of a left-handed player.

BEAT THE DEFENSE. To outwit and get by the defensemen.

BEAT THE GOALIE. To outwit and score on the goalie.

BLIND PASS. Passing the puck without looking.

BREAK. Chance to start a rush when opposing forwards are caught out of position.

BREAKAWAY. The act of a fast rush generally with no opponent between the puck-carrier and opponent's goal except the goaltender.

BREAKOUT. When the attacking team comes out of its defending zone with the puck and starts up ice.

CLEARING THE PUCK. Getting the puck away from in front of one's own goal cage area.

COVER. When a player stays close to an opponent on a play in his defensive zone, to prevent the attacker from getting free to receive a pass.

DEKE. A fake by a puck-carrier to stickhandle around an opponent.

DEFLECTION. A shot or pass that hits some object such as stick, skate, etc. and goes into the net for a score.

DIGGER. A player who relentlessly hounds the puck until he comes up with it.

DOG-A-MAN. To cover an opponent very closely and persistently.

FACE-OFF. The dropping of the puck between the sticks of two opponents to start or resume play.

FEEDING. Passing the puck.

FLOATER. An offensive player who slips into the center zone behind the attacking defensemen. Same as *hanger* or *sleeper*.

FLOPPER. A goaltender who frequently flops to the ice to make saves.

FORE CHECK. To keep opponents in their end of the rink while trying to regain control of the puck. This is usually done by the forwards.

FOREHAND. A shot or pass taken on the right side of a right-handed player, or the left side of a left-handed player.

FOUL. Any infraction of the rules that will draw a penalty.

FREEZING THE PUCK. Holding the puck against the boards with the stick or skates.

GET THE JUMP. To move fast and thereby get a good start on the opponents.

ON-THE-FLY. Making player changes or substitutions while play is under way.

OPEN ICE. That part of the ice that is free of opponents.

PLAYMAKER. The player, usually the center, who sets up the plays and gives any signals.

POINTS. The positions taken up by the defensemen on offense just inside the attacking blue line.

POWER PLAY. During a penalty, the team with the advantage sends five men with the puck into the penalized team's defending zone. Same as a *ganging play*.

PULLING THE GOALIE. Taking the goalkeeper off the ice and replacing him with a forward. Since this move leaves the goal unguarded, it is usually considered only a last-minute resort used when a team is behind and the game is practically over.

RAGGING. To retain possession of the puck by clever stickhandling.

REBOUND. A puck that bounces off the goalie's pads.

RUSH. An individual or combined attack by a team in possession of the puck.

SAVE. The act of a goalie stopping a shot.

SCRAMBLE. When several players from both sides at close range battle for possession of the puck.

SCREEN SHOT. A shot on goal from behind a screen created by either one or more players (opponents or teammates).

SHORTHANDED. A team with one or more players in the penalty box is considered shorthanded if the opponent has its *full strength* (full complement of players).

SIN-BIN. Another name for the penalty box.

SLOW WHISTLE. This is used by the linesmen when an offside occurs, without doing actual damage to the defending team's procedure. If this is so, the whistle is withheld. If then damage does occur—an unfair advantage is gained in sequence resulting from the offside—then the whistle is blown.

SOLO. A rush by a player with assistance from his teammate.

SPLITTING THE DEFENSE. Puck-carrier goes between the two opposing defensemen.

SPOT PASS. Passing to a spot rather than to a player.

TRAILER. A player who follows his teammate on the attack in position to receive a backward or drop pass.

TWO-ON-ONE. Two attacking players skating against one defensive player.

HOCKEY RULES

Official Rules printed by special permission of the National Hockey League.

SECTION TWO—TEAMS

Rule 13.   Composition of Team

(a) A team shall be composed of six players, who shall be under contract to the club they represent.

(b) Each player and each goalkeeper listed in the line-up of each team shall wear an individual identifying number at least ten inches high on the back of his sweater.

Rule 14.   Captain of Team

(a) One Captain shall be appointed by each team, and he alone shall have the privilege of discussing with the Referee any questions relating to interpretation of rules which may arise during the progress of a game. He shall wear the letter "C", approximately three inches in height and in contrasting color, in a conspicuous position on the front of his sweater.

(b) Each team should have a Captain on the ice at all times. If permanent Captain is not on the ice Alternate Captains (not more than three) shall be accorded the privileges of the Captain. Alternate Captains shall wear the letter "A", approximately three inches in height and in contrasting color, in a conspicuous place on the front of their sweaters.

(c) The Referee or Official Scorer shall be advised prior to the start of each game, the name of the Captain of the team, and also the identity of the players who will serve as Alternate Captain when the permanent Captain is off the ice.

(d) No goalkeeper shall be entitled to exercise the privileges of Captain or Alternate Captain on the ice.

(e) Only the Captain or Alternate Captain on the ice at the time of the stoppage of play (but not both) shall have the privilege of discussing with the Referee any point relating to the interpretation of rules. Any Captain, Alternate Captain or player who comes off the bench and makes any protest or intervention with the Referee for any purpose must be awarded a misconduct penalty.

   A complaint about a penalty is NOT a matter "relating to the interpretation of the rules" and a misconduct penalty shall be imposed against any Captain, Alternate Captain or other player making such a complaint.

(f) No playing Coach or playing Manager shall be permitted to act as Captain or Alternate Captain.

Rule 15.   Players in Uniform

(a) At the beginning of each game the Manager or Coach of each team shall list the players and goalkeepers who shall be eligible to play in the game. Not more than sixteen players, exclusive of goalkeepers, shall be permitted.

   In play-offs seventeen players, exclusive of goalkeepers, shall be permitted.

(b) A list of the names and numbers of all eligible players must be handed to the Referee or Official Scorer before the start of the game, and no change in the list or addition thereto shall be permitted after the commencement of the game except when a goalkeeper has been injured or becomes sick the name of another goalkeeper may be placed on the list in substitution for the injured or sick goalkeeper.

(c) Each team shall be allowed one goalkeeper on the ice at one time. The goalkeeper may be removed and another "player" substituted. Such substitute shall not be permitted the privileges of the goalkeeper.

(d) Each team shall have on, or in the immediate vicinity of its bench, a substitute goalkeeper, who shall at all times during the game be fully dressed and equipped ready to play.

   Except for the purpose of defending against a penalty shot any substitute goalkeeper entering the game for the first time shall be permitted a warm-up not exceeding two minutes. The Referee shall check the time so permitted.

(e) Except when both goalkeepers are incapacitated, no player on the playing roster in that game shall be permitted to wear the equipment of the goalkeeper.

   If both listed goalkeepers are incapacitated, that team shall be entitled to dress and play any available goalkeeper who is not on the Goalkeepers' Reserve List of any other NHL Member Club. Not more than fifteen minutes shall be allowed for such goalkeeper to be dressed and ready to play.

(f) The Referee shall report to the President for disciplinary action any delay in making a substitution of goalkeepers.

Rule 16.   Starting Line-Up

(a) Prior to the start of the game, and prior to the start of each period, at the request of the Referee, the Manager or Coach of the visiting team is required to name the starting line-up to the Referee or the Official Scorer. At any time in the game at the request of the Referee, made to the Captain or Alternate Captain, the visiting team must place a playing line-up on the ice and promptly commence play.

(b) Prior to the start of the game the Manager or Coach of the home team, having been advised by the Official Scorer or the Referee the names of the starting line-up of the visiting team, shall name the starting line-up of the home team which information shall be conveyed by the Official Scorer or the Referee to the Coach of the visiting team.

(c) No change in the starting line-up either team as given to the Referee or Official Scorer, or in the playing line-up on the ice, shall be made until the game is actually in progress. For an infraction of this rule a bench minor penalty shall be imposed upon the offending team, provided such infraction is called to the attention of the Referee before the second face-off in the period takes place.

(d) Only players who will participate in the initial face-off will be allowed on the ice before the start of the second and third periods.

Rule 17. Equalizing of Teams

D E L E T E D

Rule 18. Change of Players

(a) Players may be changed at any time from the players' bench, provided that the player or players leaving the ice shall always be at the players' bench and out of the play before any change is made.

A goalkeeper may be changed for another player at any time under the conditions set out in this section.

(NOTE) *When a goalkeeper leaves his goal area and proceeds to his players' bench for the purpose of substituting another player, the rear Linesman shall be responsible to see that the substitution made is not illegal by reason of the premature departure of the substitute from the bench (before the goalkeeper is within ten feet of the bench). If the substitution is made prematurely, the Linesman shall stop the play immediately by blowing his whistle. There shall be no time penalty to the team making the premature substitution but the resulting face-off will take place on the center "face-off spot."*

(b) If, by reason of insufficient playing time remaining, or by reason of penalties already imposed for deliberate illegal substitution (too many men on the ice) which cannot be served in its entirety within the legal playing time, a penalty shot shall be awarded against the offending team.

(c) A player serving a penalty on the penalty bench, who is to be changed after the penalty has been served, must proceed at once by way of the ice and be at his own players' bench before any change can be made.

For any violation of this rule a bench minor penalty shall be imposed.

Rule 19. Injured Players

(a) When a player, other than a goalkeeper, is injured or compelled to leave the ice during a game, he may retire from the game and be replaced by a substitute, but play must continue without the teams leaving the ice.

(b) If a goalkeeper sustains an injury or becomes ill he must be ready to resume play immediately or be replaced by a substitute goalkeeper and NO additional time shall be allowed by the referee for the purpose of enabling the injured or ill goalkeeper to resume his position. (See also Section (d)).

(c) The Referee shall report to the President for disciplinary action any delay in making a goalkeeper substitution.

The substitute goalkeeper shall be subject to the regular rules governing goalkeepers and shall be entitled to the same privileges.

(d) When a substitution for the regular goalkeeper has been made, such regular goalkeeper shall not resume his position until the first stoppage of play thereafter. When the substitute goalkeeper comes on the ice and starts his warm-up he shall complete it and shall not be allowed any additional warm up in the same game.

(e) If a penalized player has been injured he may proceed to the dressing room without the necessity of taking a seat on the penalty bench. If the injured player receives a minor penalty the penalized team shall immediately put a substitute player on the penalty bench who shall serve the penalty without change. If the injured player receives a major penalty the penalized team shall place a substitute player on the penalty bench before the penalty expires and no other replacement for the penalized player shall be permitted to enter the game except from the penalty bench. For violation of this rule a bench minor penalty shall be imposed.

The penalized player who has been injured and been replaced on the penalty bench shall not be eligible to play until his penalty has expired.

(f) When a player is injured so that he cannot continue play or go to his bench, the play shall not be stopped until the injured player's team has secured possession of the puck; if the player's team is in possession of the puck at the time of injury, play shall be stopped immediately, unless his team is in a scoring position.

(NOTE) *In the case where it is obvious that a player has sustained a serious injury the Referee may stop the play immediately.*

SECTION FOUR—PENALTIES

Rule 26. Penalties

Penalties shall be actual playing time and shall be divided into the following classes:
- (1) Minor Penalties
- (2) Bench Minor Penalties
- (3) Major Penalties
- (4) Misconduct Penalties
- (5) Match Penalties
- (6) Penalty Shot.

Where coincident penalties are imposed on players of both teams the penalized players of the visiting team shall take their positions on the penalty bench first in the place designated for visiting players, or where there is no special designation then on the bench farthest from the gate.

(NOTE) *When play is not actually in progress and an offense is committed by any player, the same penalty shall apply as though play were actually in progress. Accidental trips occurring simultaneously with, or after, stoppage of play will not be penalized.*

Rule 27. Minor Penalties

(a) For a "MINOR PENALTY," any player, other than a goalkeeper, shall be ruled off the ice for two minutes during which time no substitute shall be permitted.

(b) A "BENCH MINOR" penalty involves the removal from the ice of one player of the team against which the penalty is awarded for a period of two minutes. Any player of the team may be designated to serve the penalty by the Manager or Coach through the playing Captain and such player shall take his place on the penalty bench promptly and serve the penalty as if it was a minor penalty imposed upon him.

(c) If while a team is "short-handed" by one or more minor or bench minor penalties the opposing team scores a goal, the first of such penalties shall automatically terminate.

(NOTE 1) *"Short-handed" means that the team must be below the numerical strength of its opponents on the ice at the time the goal is scored. The minor or bench minor penalty which terminates automatically is the one which causes the team scored against to be "short-handed" originally (first penalty). Thus coincident minor penalties to both teams do NOT cause either side to be "short-handed."*

This rule shall also apply when a goal is scored on a penalty shot.

When the minor penalties of two players of the same team terminate at the same time the Captain of that team shall designate to the Referee which of such players will return to the ice first and the Referee will instruct the Penalty Timekeeper accordingly.

When a player receives a major penalty and a minor penalty at the same time the major penalty shall be served first by the penalized player except under Rule 28 (f) in which case the minor penalty will be recorded and served first.

(NOTE 2) : *This applies to the case where BOTH penalties are imposed on the SAME player.*

See also Note to Rule 33.

Rule 28.   Major Penalties

(a) For the first "MAJOR PENALTY" in any one game, the offender, except the goalkeeper, shall be ruled off the ice for five minutes, during which time no substitute shall be permitted.

An automatic fine of twenty-five dollars ($25.00) shall also be added when a major penalty is imposed for any foul causing injury to the face or head of an opponent by means of a stick.

(b) For the second major penalty in the same game, to the same player, except the goalkeeper, he shall be ruled off the ice for fifteen minutes, but substitute shall be permitted after five minutes have elapsed. (Major penalty plus misconduct penalty with automatic fine of twenty-five dollars ($25.00).

(c) For the third major penalty in the same game, to the same player, he shall be ruled off the ice for the balance of the playing time, but a substitute shall be permitted to replace the player so suspended after five minutes shall have elapsed. (Major penalty plus game misconduct penalty with automatic fine of fifty dollars ($50.00).

(d) When coincident major penalties are imposed against an equal number of players of each team, the penalized players shall all take their places on the penalty benches and such penalized players shall not leave the penalty bench until the first stoppage of play following the expiry of their respective penalties. Immediate substitutions shall be made for the players so penalized and their penalties shall not be taken into account for the purpose of the delayed penalty Rule 33.

(e) When coincident penalties of equal duration including a major penalty are imposed upon a player of each team, the penalized players shall take their places on the penalty bench and such players shall not leave the penalty bench until the first stoppage of play following the expiry of their respective penalties. Immediate substitutions shall be made for the players so penalized and their penalties shall not be taken into account for the purpose of the delayed penalty Rule 33 or Rule 27 (c).

(f) When coincident penalties of unequal duration (each including one major penalty) are imposed upon a player of each team the penalized players shall take their places on the penalty bench and such players shall not leave the penalty bench until the first stoppage of play following the expiry of their respective penalties.

The penalties which created the disparity in total penalty time between the players penalized affected shall be served first in the normal way by the players penalized. Immediate substitution shall be permitted for the major penalties of each player.

Account shall be taken of the penalties which create the disparity in the total penalty time awarded to the players affected for the purposes of the delayed penalty Rule 33 and for Rule 27 (c) (goal scored against a short-handed team).

Rule 29.   Misconduct Penalties

(a) "MISCONDUCT" penalties to all players except the goalkeeper, involve removal from the game for a period of ten minutes each. A substitute player is permitted to immediately replace a player serving a misconduct penalty. A player whose mis-

conduct penalty has expired shall remain in the penalty box until the next stoppage of play.

When a player receives a minor penalty and a misconduct penalty at the same time, the penalized team shall immediately put a substitute player on the penalty bench and he shall serve the minor penalty without change.

When a player receives a major penalty and a misconduct penalty at the same time, the penalized team shall place a substitute player on the penalty bench before the major penalty expires and no replacement for the penalized player shall be permitted to enter the game except from the penalty bench. Any violation of this provision shall be treated as an illegal substitution under Rule 18 calling for a bench minor penalty.

(b) A misconduct penalty imposed on any player at any time, shall be accompanied with an automatic fine of twenty-five dollars ($25.00).

(c) A "GAME MISCONDUCT" penalty involves the suspension of a player for the balance of the game but a substitute is permitted to replace immediately the player so removed. A player incurring a game misconduct penalty shall incur an automatic fine of fifty dollars ($50.00) and his case shall be reported to the President who shall have full power to impose such further penalty by way of suspension or fine as he may deem fitting.

(NOTE) *For all "Game Misconduct" penalties regardless of when imposed, a total of ten minutes shall be charged in the records against the offending player.*

Rule 30.   Match Penalties

(a) A "MATCH" penalty involves the suspension of a player for the balance of the game, and the offender shall be ordered to the dressing room immediately. A substitute player is permitted to replace the penalized player after ten minutes playing time has elapsed when the penalty is imposed under Rule 49, and after five minutes actual playing time has elapsed when the penalty is imposed under Rule 44 or Rule 64.

(NOTE) *Regulations regarding additional penalties and substitutes are specifically covered in individual Rules 44, 49 and 64; any additional penalty shall be served by a player to be designated by the Manager or Coach of the offending team through the playing Captain.*

(NOTE 2) When coincident match penalties have been imposed under Rule 44 or Rule 64 to a player on both teams Rule 28 (d) and (f) covering coincident major penalties will not be applicable.

For all "MATCH" penalties, regardless of when imposed, or prescribed additional penalties, a total of ten minutes shall be charged in the records against the offending player.

(b) A player incurring a match penalty shall incur an automatic fine of one hundred dollars ($100.00) and his case shall be investigated promptly by the President who shall have full power to impose such further penalty by way of suspension or fine as he may deem fitting.

Rule 31.   Penalty Shot

(a) Any infraction of the rules which calls for a "Penalty Shot" shall be taken as follows : —

The Referee shall cause to be announced over the public address system the name of the player designated by him or selected by the team entitled to take the shot (as appropriate) and shall then place the puck on the center face-off spot and the player taking the shot will, on the instruction of the Referee, play the puck from there and shall attempt to score on the goalkeeper. The player taking the shot may carry the puck in any part of the Neutral Zone or his own Defending Zone but once the puck has crossed the Attacking Blue Line it must be kept in motion towards the opponent's goal line and once it is shot the play shall be considered complete. No goal can be scored on a rebound of any kind and any time the puck crosses the goal line the shot shall be considered complete.

(b) The goalkeeper must remain in his goal crease until the puck has crossed the adjacent Blue Line and, in the event of violation of this rule, the player designated or selected to take the shot shall be entitled to take the shot over again.

The goalkeeper may attempt to stop the shot in any manner except by throwing his stick or any other object, in which case a goal shall be awarded.

(NOTE) *See Rule 80.*

(c) In cases where a penalty shot has been awarded under Rule 66(h) — for illegal entry into the game, under Rule 80(a) — for throwing a stick and under Rule 83(b) — for fouling from behind, the Referee shall designate the player who has been fouled as the player who shall take the penalty shot.

In cases where a penalty shot has been awarded under Rule 53 (c) — falling on the puck in the crease or Rule 57 (d) — picking up the puck from the crease area—the penalty shot shall be taken by a player selected by the Captain of the non-offending team from the players on the ice at the time when the foul was committed. Such selection shall be reported to the Referee and cannot be changed.

If by reason of injury the player designated by the Referee to take the penalty shot is unable to do so within a reasonable time, the shot may be taken by a player selected by the Captain of the non-offending team from the players on the ice when the foul was committed. Such selection shall be reported to the Referee and cannot be changed.

(d) Should the player in respect to whom a penalty shot has been awarded himself commit a foul in connection with the same play or circumstances, either before or after the penalty shot penalty has been awarded, be designated to take the shot, he shall first be permitted to do so before being sent to the penalty bench to serve the penalty.

If at the time a penalty shot is awarded the goalkeeper of the penalized team has been removed from the ice to substitute another player the goalkeeper shall be permitted to return to the ice before the penalty shot is taken.

(e) While the penalty shot is being taken, players of both sides shall withdraw to the sides of the rink and beyond the center red line.

(f) If, while the penalty shot is being taken, any player of the opposing team shall have by some action interfered with or distracted the player taking the shot and because of such action the shot should have failed, a second attempt shall be permitted and the Referee shall impose a misconduct penalty on the player so interfering or distracting.

(g) If a goal is scored from a penalty shot the puck shall be faced at center ice in the usual way. If a goal is not scored the puck shall be faced at either of the end face-off spots in the zone in which the penalty shot has been tried.

(h) Should a goal be scored from a penalty shot, a further penalty to the offending player shall not be applied unless the offense for which the penalty shot was awarded was such as to incur a major or match penalty, in which case the penalty prescribed for the particular offense, shall be imposed.

If the offense for which the penalty shot was awarded was such as would normally incur a minor penalty, then regardless of whether the penalty shot results in a goal or not, no further minor penalty shall be served.

(i) If the foul upon which the penalty shot is based occurs during actual playing time the penalty shot shall be awarded and taken immediately in the usual manner notwithstanding any delay occasioned by a slow whistle by the Referee to permit the play to be completed which delay results in the expiry of the regular playing time in any period.

The time required for the taking of a penalty shot shall not be included in the regular playing time or any overtime.

Rule 32. Goalkeeper's Penalties

(a) A goalkeeper shall not be sent to the penalty bench for an offense which incurs a minor penalty, but instead the minor penalty shall be served by a player to be designated by the Manager or Coach of the offending team through the playing Captain and such substitute shall not be changed.

(b) A goalkeeper shall not be sent to the penalty bench for an infraction of the rules which would call for a major penalty, but instead the major penalty shall be served by a player to be designated by the Manager or Coach of the offending team through the playing Captain and such substitute shall not be changed.

(c) Should a goalkeeper incur a second major penalty in one game, for the second offense he will also receive a game misconduct penalty, and his place will be taken by a member of his own club, or by a regular substitute goalkeeper who is available. (Major penalty plus Game Misconduct penalty, and automatic fine of fifty dollars $50.00).

(d) Should a goalkeeper incur a misconduct penalty, this penalty shall be served by another member of his team who was on the ice when the offense was committed, said player to be designated by the Manager or Coach of the offending team through the playing Captain; and in addition the goalkeeper shall be fined twenty-five dollars ($25.00).

(e) Should a goalkeeper incur a game misconduct penalty, his place then will be taken by a member of his own club, or by a regular substitute goalkeeper who is available, and such player will be allowed the goalkeeper's full equipment. In addition, the goalkeeper shall be fined fifty dollars ($50.00).

(f) Should a goalkeeper incur a match penalty, his place then will be taken by a member of his own club, or by a substitute goalkeeper who is available, and such player will be allowed the goalkeeper's equipment. However, any additional penalties as specifically called for by the individual rules covering match penalties, will apply, and the offending team shall be penalized accordingly; such additional penalty to be served by another member of the team on the ice at the time the offense was committed, said player to be designated by the Manager or Coach of the offending team through the playing Captain. (See Rules 44, 49 and 64).

(g) A goalkeeper incurring a match penalty shall incur an automatic fine of one hundred dollars ($100.00) and his case shall be investigated promptly by the President who shall have full power to impose such further penalty by way of suspension or fine as he may deem fitting.

(h) When a goalkeeper leaves the immediate vicinity of his goal crease and takes part in any altercation he shall be subject to a fine of fifty dollars ($50.00) without a time penalty.

(NOTE) *All penalties imposed on goalkeeper regardless of who serves penalty or any substitution, shall be charged in the records against the goalkeeper.*

(i) If a goalkeeper participates in the play in any manner when he is beyond the center red line a minor penalty shall be imposed upon him.

Rule 33. Delayed Penalties

(a) If a third player of any team shall be penalized while two players of the same team are serving penalties, the penalty time of the third player shall not commence until the penalty time of one of the two players already penalized shall have elapsed. Nevertheless, the third player penalized must at once proceed to the penalty bench but may be replaced by a substitute until such time as the penalty time of the penalized player shall commence.

(b) When any team shall have three players serving penalties at the same time and because of the delayed penalty rule, a substitute for the third offender is on the ice, none of the three penalized players on the penalty bench may return to the ice until play has been stopped. When play has been stopped, the player whose full penalty has expired, may return to the play.

Provided however that the Penalty Timekeeper shall permit the return to the ice in the order of expiry of their penalties, of a player or players when by reason of the expiration of their penalties the penalized team is entitled to have more than four players on the ice.

(c) In the case of delayed penalties, the Referee shall instruct the Penalty Timekeeper that penalized players whose penalties have expired shall only be allowed to return to the ice when there is a stoppage of play.

When the penalties of two players of the same team will expire at the same time the Captain of that team will designate to the Referee which of such players will return to the ice first, and the Referee will instruct the Penalty Timekeeper accordingly.

When a major and a minor penalty are imposed at the same time on players of the same team the Penalty Timekeeper shall record the minor as being the first of such penalties.

(NOTE) *This applies to the case where the two penalties are imposed on DIFFERENT players of the same team. See also Note to Rule 27.*

Rule 34. Calling of Penalties

(a) Should an infraction of the rules which would call for a minor, major or match penalty be committed by a player of the side in possession of the puck, the Referee shall immediately blow his whistle and give the penalties to the deserving players.

The resulting face-off shall be made at the place where the play was stopped unless the stoppage occurs in the Attacking Zone of the player penalized in which case the face-off shall be made at the nearest face-off spot in the Neutral Zone.

(b) Should an infraction of the rules which would call for a minor, major or match penalty be committed by a player of the team NOT in possession of the puck, the Referee shall signify the calling of a penalty by pointing to the offending player, and on completion of the play by the team in possession, will immediately blow his whistle and give the penalty to the deserving player.

The resulting face-off shall be made at the place where the play was stopped, unless during the period of a delayed whistle due to a foul by a player of the side NOT in possession, the side in possession ices the puck, shoots the puck so that it goes out of bounds or is unplayable then the face-off following the stoppage shall take place in the Neutral Zone near the Defending Blue Line of the team shooting the puck.

If the penalty to be imposed is a minor penalty, and a goal is scored on the play *by the non-offending side* the minor penalty shall not be imposed but major and match penalties shall be imposed in the normal manner regardless of whether a goal is scored or not.

(NOTE 1) *"Completion of the play by the team in possession" in this rule means that the puck must have come into the possession and control of an opposing player or has been "frozen." This does not mean a rebound off the goalkeeper, the goal or the boards or any accidental contact with the body or equipment of an opposing player.*

(NOTE 2) *If after the Referee has signalled a penalty but before the whistle has been blown the puck shall enter the goal of the non-offending team as the direct result of the action of a player of that team, the goal shall be allowed and the penalty signalled shall be imposed in the normal manner.*

If when a team is "short-handed" by reason of one or more minor or bench minor penalties the Referee signals a further minor penalty against the "short-handed" team and a goal is scored by the non-offending side before the whistle is blown then the goal shall be allowed, the penalty signalled shall be washed out and the first of the minor penalties already being served shall automatically terminate under Rule 27 (c).

(c) Should the same offending player commit other fouls on the same play, either before or after the Referee has blown his whistle, the offending player shall serve such penalties consecutively.

SECTION SIX—PLAYING RULES

Rule 42. Abuse of Officials and other Misconduct

(NOTE) *In the enforcement of this rule the Referee has, in many instances, the option of imposing a "misconduct penalty" or a "bench minor penalty." In principle the Referee is directed to impose a "bench minor penalty" in respect to the violations which occur on or in the immediate vicinity of the players' bench but off the playing surface, and in all cases affecting non-playing personnel or players. A "misconduct penalty" should be imposed for violations which occur on the playing surface or in the penalty bench area and where the penalized player is readily identifiable.*

(a) A misconduct penalty shall be imposed on any player who uses obscene, profane or abusive language or gestures to any person or who persists in disputing or shows disrespect for the rulings of any official during a game or who intentionally knocks or shoots the puck out of the reach of an official who is retrieving it.

(b) A misconduct penalty shall be imposed on any player or players who bang the boards with their sticks or other instruments any time.

(c) A misconduct penalty shall be imposed on any penalized player who does not proceed directly and immediately to the penalty box and take his place on the penalty bench.

Where coincident penalties are imposed on players of both teams the penalized players of the visiting team shall take their positions on the penalty bench first in the place designated for visiting players, or where there is no special designation then on the bench farthest from the gate.

Any player who (following a fight or other altercation in which he has been involved is broken up, and for which he is penalized) fails to proceed immediately to the penalty bench or who persists in continuing or attempting to continue the fight or altercation or who resists a Linesman in the discharge of his duties shall incur an automatic fine of $50.00 in addition to all other penalties or fines incurred.

(d) A misconduct penalty shall be imposed on any player who, after warning by the Referee, persists in any course of conduct (including threatening or abusive language or gestures or similar actions) designed to incite an opponent into incurring a penalty.

(e) In the case of any Club Executive, Manager, Coach or Trainer being guilty of such misconduct, he is to be removed from the bench by order of the Referee, and his case reported to the President for further action.

(f) If any Club Executive, Manager, Coach or Trainer is removed from the bench by order of the Referee, he must not sit near the bench of his club, nor in any way direct or attempt to direct the play of his club.

(g) A bench minor penalty shall be imposed against the offending team if any player, any Club Executive, Manager, Coach or Trainer uses obscene, profane or abusive language to any person or uses the name of any official coupled with any vociferous remarks.

(h) A bench minor penalty shall be imposed against the offending team if any player, Trainer, Coach, Manager or Club Executive in the vicinity of the players' bench or penalty bench throws anything on the ice during the progress of the game or during stoppage of play.

(i) A bench minor penalty shall be imposed against the offending team if any player, Trainer, Coach, Manager or Club Executive interferes in any manner with any game official including Referee, Linesmen, Timekeepers or Goal Judges in the performance of their duties.

The Referee may assess further penalties under Rule 67 (Molesting Officials) if he deems them to be warranted.

(j) A misconduct penalty shall be imposed on any player or players who, except for the purpose of taking their positions on the penalty bench, enter or remain in the Referee's Crease while he is reporting to or consulting with any game official including Linesmen, Timekeeper, Penalty Timekeeper, Official Scorer or Announcer.

Rule 43. Adjustment to Clothing and Equipment

(a) Play shall not be stopped, nor the game delayed by reason of adjustments to clothing, equipment shoes, skates or sticks.

(b) For an infringement of this rule, a minor penalty shall be given.

(c) The onus of maintaining clothing and equipment in proper condition shall be upon the player. If adjustments are required, the player shall retire from the ice and play shall continue uninterruptedly with a substitute.

(d) However a goalkeeper, after a stoppage of play, with the permission of the Referee, may be allowed to make adjustments or repairs to clothing, equipment, shoes or skates.

A goalkeeper may also be permitted by the Referee to replace his mask but no time shall be allowed for repair or fitting of a mask.

(e) For an infraction of the rule by a goalkeeper, a minor penalty shall be imposed.

Rule 44.   Attempt to Injure

A match penalty shall be imposed on any player who deliberately attempts to injure an opponent, official, Manager, Coach, or Trainer in any manner, and the circumstances shall be reported to the President for further action. A substitute for the penalized player shall be permitted at the end of the fifth minute.

Rule 45.   Board-Checking

A minor or major penalty, at the discretion of the Referee based upon the degree of violence of the impact with the boards, shall be imposed on any player who body-checks, cross-checks, elbows, charges or trips an opponent in such a manner that causes the opponent to be thrown violently into the boards.

(NOTE) *Any unnecessary contact with a player playing the puck on an obvious "icing" or "off-side" play which results in that player being knocked into the fence is "boarding" and must be penalized as such. In other instances where there is no contact with the fence it should be treated as "charging."*

"Rolling" an opponent (if he is the puck carrier) along the fence where he is endeavouring to go through too small an opening is not boarding. However, if the opponent is not the puck carrier, then such action should be penalized as boarding, charging, interference or if the arms or stick are employed it should be called holding or hooking.

Rule 46   Broken Stick

(a) A player without a stick may participate in the game. A player whose stick is broken may participate in the game provided he drops the broken portion. A minor penalty shall be imposed for an infraction of this rule.

(NOTE) *A broken stick is one which, in the opinion of the Referee, is unfit for normal play.*

(b) A goalkeeper may continue to play with a broken stick until stoppage of play or until he has been legally provided with a stick.

(c) A player whose stick is broken may not receive a stick thrown on the ice from any part of the rink but must obtain same at his players' bench. A goalkeeper whose stick is broken may not receive a stick thrown on the ice from any part of the rink but may receive a stick from a teammate without proceeding to his players' bench. A minor penalty plus a misconduct penalty shall be imposed on the player or goalkeeper receiving a stick illegally under this rule.

Rule 47.   Charging

(a) A minor or major penalty shall be imposed on a player who runs or jumps into or charges an opponent.

(b) A minor or major penalty shall be imposed on a player who charges a goalkeeper while the goalkeeper is within his goal crease.

(NOTE) *If more than two steps or strides are taken it shall be considered a charge.*

A goalkeeper is NOT "fair game" just because he is outside the goal crease area. A penalty for interference or charging (minor or major) should be called in every case where an opposing player makes unnecessary contact with a goalkeeper.

Likewise Referees should be alert to penalize goalkeepers for tripping, slashing or spearing in the vicinity of the goal.

Rule 48.   Cross-Checking and Butt-Ending

(a) A minor or major penalty, at the discretion of the Referee, shall be imposed on a player who "cross-checks" or "butt-ends" an opponent.

(b) A minor or major penalty shall be imposed on a player who "cross-checks" or "butt-ends" a goalkeeper while the goalkeeper is within his goal crease.

(c) A major penalty shall be imposed on any player who injures an opponent by "cross-checking" or "butt-ending."

When a major penalty is imposed under this rule for a foul resulting in injury to the face or head of an opponent, an automatic fine of twenty-five dollars ($25.00) shall also be imposed.

(NOTE) *Cross-check shall mean a check delivered with both hands on the stick and no part of the stick on the ice.*

Rule 49. Deliberate Injury of Opponents

(a) A match penalty shall be imposed on a player who deliberately injures an opponent in any manner.

(b) In addition to the match penalty, the Referee shall impose a fine of one hundred dollars ($100.00) on any player who deliberately injures another in any manner.

(c) No substitute shall be permitted to take the place of the penalized player until ten minutes actual playing time shall have elapsed, from the time the penalty was imposed.

Rule 50. Delaying the Game

(a) No player or goalkeeper shall delay the game by deliberately shooting or batting the puck outside the playing area. The Referee shall report every such incident to the President for disciplinary action.

The Referee shall impose a minor penalty, immediately and without warning, against any player or goalkeeper who throws the puck outside the playing area.

(b) A minor penalty shall be imposed on any player (including goalkeeper) who delays the game by deliberately displacing a goal post from its normal position.

If by reason of insufficient time in the regular playing time or by reason of penalties already imposed the minor penalty awarded for an offense under this section cannot be served in its entirety within the regular playing time of the game, a penalty shot shall be awarded against the offending team.

(c) A bench minor penalty shall be imposed upon any team which, after warning by the Referee to its Captain or Alternate Captain to place the correct number of players on the ice and commence play, fails to comply with the Referee's direction and thereby causes any delay by making additional substitutions, by persisting in having its players off-side, or in any other manner.

Rule 51. Elbowing and Kneeing

(a) A minor penalty shall be imposed on any player who uses his elbow or knee in such a manner as to in any way foul an opponent.

(b) A major penalty shall be imposed on any player who injures an opponent as the result of a foul committed by using his elbow or knee.

Rule 52. Face-Offs

(a) The puck shall be "faced-off" by the Referee or the Linesman dropping the puck on the ice between the sticks of the players "facing-off." Players facing-off will stand squarely facing their opponents' end of the rink approximately one stick length apart with the full blade of their sticks on the ice.

When the face-off takes place in any of the end face-off circles the players taking part shall take their positions so that they will have one skate on each side and clear of the line running through the face-off spot and with both feet behind and clear of the line parallel to the goal line. The sticks of both players facing-off shall have the full blade on the ice and entirely clear of the spot or place where the puck is to be dropped.

No other player shall be allowed to enter the face-off circle or come within fifteen feet of the players facing-off the puck, and must stand on side on all face-offs.

If a violation of this subsection of this rule occurs the Referee or Linesman shall re-face the puck.

(NOTE) *If after warning by the Referee or Linesman either of the players fails to take his proper position for the face-off promptly, the official shall be entitled to face-off the puck notwithstanding such default.*

(b) In the conduct of any face-off anywhere on the playing surface no player facing-off shall make any physical contact with his opponent's body by means of his own body or by his stick except in the course of playing the puck after the face-off has been completed.

For violation of this rule the Referee shall impose a minor penalty or penalties on the player(s) whose action(s) caused the physical contact.

(NOTE) *"Conduct of any face-off" commences when the Referee designates the place of the face-off and he (or the Linesman) takes up his position to drop the puck.*

(c) If a player facing-off fails to take his proper position immediately when directed by the Official, the Official may order him replaced for that face-off by any teammate then on the ice.

(d) A second violation of any of the provisions of sub-section (a) hereof during the same face-off shall be penalized with a minor penalty to the player who commits the second violation of the rule.

(e) When an infringement of a rule has been committed or a stoppage of play has been caused by any player of the attacking side in the Attacking Zone the ensuing face-off shall be made in the Neutral Zone on the nearest face-off spot.

(NOTE) *This includes stoppage of play caused by player of attacking side shooting the puck on to the back of the defending team's net without any intervening action by the defending team.*

(f) When an infringement of a rule has been committed by players of both sides in the play resulting in the stoppage, the ensuing face-off will be made at the place of such infringement or at the place where play is stopped in cases where play is permitted to be completed, unless otherwise expressly provided by these rules.

(g) When stoppage occurs between the end face-off spots and near end of rink the puck shall be faced-off at the end face-off spot, on the side where the stoppage occurs unless otherwise expressly provided by these rules.

(h) No face-off shall be made within fifteen feet of the goal or sideboards.

(i) When a goal is illegally scored as a result of a puck being deflected directly from an official anywhere in the defending zone (if the puck was last in possession of a defending player) the resulting face-off shall be made at the end face-off spot in the defending zone.

(j) When the game is stopped for any reason not specifically covered in the official rules, the puck must be faced-off where it was last played.

(k) The whistle will not be blown by the official to start play. Playing time will commence from the instant the puck is faced-off and will stop when the whistle is blown.

Rule 53. Falling on Puck

(a) A minor penalty shall be imposed on a player other than the goalkeeper who deliberately falls on or gathers a puck into his body.

(NOTE) *Defencemen who drop to their knees to block shots should not be penalized if the puck is shot under them or becomes lodged in their clothing or equipment but any use of the hands to make the puck unplayable should be penalized promptly.*

(b) A minor penalty shall be imposed on a goalkeeper who (when his body is entirely outside the boundaries of his own crease area and when the puck is behind the goal line) deliberately falls on or gathers the puck into his body or who holds or places the puck against any part of the goal or against the boards.

(c) No defending player, except the goalkeeper, will be permitted to fall on the puck or hold the puck or gather a puck into the body or hands when the puck is within the goal crease.

For infringement of this rule, play shall immediately be stopped and a penalty shot shall be ordered against the offending team, but no other penalty shall be given.

(NOTE) *This rule shall be interpreted so that a penalty shot will be awarded only when the puck is in the crease at the instant the play is stopped. However, in cases where the puck is outside the crease, Rule 53 (a) may still apply and a minor penalty may be imposed, even though no penalty shot is awarded.*

Rule 54. Fisticuffs

(a) A major, double minor or minor penalty at the discretion of the Referee, shall be imposed on any player who starts fisticuffs.

(b) A minor penalty shall be imposed on a player who, having been struck, shall retaliate with a blow or attempted blow. However, at the discretion of the Referee a major or a double minor penalty may be imposed if such player continues the altercation.

(NOTE) *The Referee is provided very wide latitude in the penalties which he may impose under this rule. This is done intentionally to enable him to differentiate between the obvious degrees of responsibility of the participants either for starting the fighting or persisting in continuing the fighting. The discretion provided should be exercised realistically.*

(NOTE 2) *Referees are directed to employ every means provided by these Rules to stop "brawling" and should use Rule 42 (c) for this purpose.*

(c) A misconduct penalty shall be imposed on any player involved in fisticuffs off the playing surface or with another player who is off the playing surface.

Rule 55. Goals and Assists

(NOTE) *It is the responsibility of the Official Scorer to award goals and assists, and his decision in this respect is final notwithstanding the report of the Referee or any other game official. Such awards shall be made or withheld strictly in accordance with the provisions of this rule. Therefore, it is essential that the Official Scorer shall be thoroughly familiar with every aspect of this rule, be alert to observe all actions which could affect the making of an award and, above all, the awards must be made or withheld with absolute impartiality.*

In case of an obvious error in awarding a goal or an assist which has been announced, it should be corrected promptly but changes should not be made in the official scoring summary after the Referee has signed the Game Report.

(a) A goal shall be scored when the puck shall have been put between the goal posts by the stick of a player of the attacking side, from in front, and below the cross bar, and entirely across a red line, the width of the diameter of the goal posts drawn on the ice from one goal post to the other.

(b) A goal shall be scored if the puck is put into the goal in any way by a player of the defending side.

The player of the attacking side who last played the puck shall be credited with the goal but no assist shall be awarded.

(c) If an attacking player kicks the puck and it is deflected into the net by any player of the defending side except the goalkeeper, the goal shall be allowed. The player who kicked the puck shall be credited with the goal but no assist shall be awarded.

(d) If the puck shall have been deflected into the goal from the shot of an attacking player by striking any part of the person of a player of the same side, a goal shall be allowed. The player who deflected the puck shall be credited with the goal. The goal shall not be allowed if the puck has been kicked, thrown or otherwise deliberately directed into the goal by any means other than a stick.

(e) If a goal is scored as a result of a puck being deflected directly into the net from an official the goal shall not be allowed.

(f) Should a player legally propel a puck into the goal crease of the opponent club and the puck should become loose and available to another player of the attacking side, a goal scored on the play shall be legal.

(g) Any goal scored, other than as covered by the official rules, shall not be allowed.

(h) A "goal" shall be credited in the scoring records to a player who shall have propelled the puck into the opponents' goal. Each "goal" shall count one point in the player's record.

(i) When a player scores a goal an "assist" shall be credited to the player or players taking part in the play immediately preceding the goal, but not more than two assists can be given on any goal. Each "assist" so credited shall count one point in the player's record.

(j) Only one point can be credited to any one player on a goal.

Rule 56. Gross Misconduct

(a) The Referee may suspend from the game and order to the dressing room for the remainder of the game, any player, Manager, Coach or Trainer guilty of gross misconduct of any kind.

(b) If a player so dismissed is taking part in the game, he shall be charged with a game misconduct penalty, and a substitute shall be permitted.

(c) The Referee in charge is to decide on any violation and report the incident to the President of the League for further action.

Rule 57. Handling Puck With Hands

(a) If a player, except the goalkeeper, closes his hand on the puck the play shall be stopped and a minor penalty shall be imposed on him. A goalkeeper who holds the puck with his hands for longer than three seconds shall be given a minor penalty.

(b) A goalkeeper must not deliberately hold the puck in any manner which in the opinion of the Referee causes a stoppage of play, nor throw the puck forward towards the opponents' goal, nor deliberately drop the puck into his pads or on to the goal net, nor deliberately pile up snow or obstacles at or near his net, that in the opinion of the Referee would tend to prevent the scoring of a goal.

(NOTE) *The object of this entire rule is to keep the puck in play continuously and any action taken by the goalkeeper which causes an unnecessary stoppage must be penalized without warning.*

(c) The penalty for infringement of this rule by the goalkeeper shall be a minor penalty.

(NOTE) *In the case of puck thrown forward by the goalkeeper being taken by an opponent, the Referee shall allow the resulting play to be completed, and if a goal is scored by the non-offending team, it shall be allowed and no penalty given; but if a goal is not scored, play shall be stopped and a minor penalty shall be awarded against the goalkeeper*

(d) A minor penalty shall be imposed on a player except the goalkeeper who, while play is in progress, picks up the puck off the ice with his hand.

If a player, except the goalkeeper, while play in progress, picks up the puck with his hand, from the ice in the goal crease area the play shall be stopped immediately and a penalty shot shall be awarded to the non-offending team.

(e) A player shall be permitted to stop or "bat" a puck in the air with his open hand, or push it along the ice with his hand, and the play shall not be stopped unless in the opinion of the Referee he has deliberately directed the puck to a teammate, in which case the play shall be stopped and the puck faced-off at the spot where the offense occurred.

(NOTE) *The object of this rule is to ensure continuous action and the Referee should NOT stop play unless he is satisfied that the directing of the puck to a teammate was in fact DELIBERATE.*

The puck may not be "batted" with the hand directly into the net at any time, but a goal shall be allowed when the puck has been legally "batted" and is deflected into the goal by a defending player except the goalkeeper.

Rule 58.　　　　High Sticks

(a) The carrying of sticks above the normal height of the shoulder is prohibited, and a minor penalty may be imposed on any player violating this rule, at the discretion of the Referee.

(b) A goal scored from a stick so carried shall not be allowed, except by a player of the defending team.

(c) When a player carries or holds any part of his stick above the height of his shoulder so that injury to the face or head of an opposing player results, the Referee shall have no alternative but to impose a major penalty on the offending player.

When a major penalty is imposed under this rule for a foul resulting in injury to the face or head of an opponent, an automatic fine of twenty-five dollars ($25.00) shall also be imposed.

(d) Batting the puck above the normal height of the shoulders with the stick is prohibited and when it occurs there shall be a Whistle and ensuing face-off at the spot where the offense occurred unless :
1. the defending player in his own Defending Zone or in the Neutral Zone shall bat the puck to an opponent in which case the play shall continue, or
2. a player of the defending side shall bat the puck into his own goal in which case the goal shall be allowed.

(NOTE) *When player bats the puck to an opponent under subsection 1 the Referee shall give the "wash-out" signal immediately. Otherwise he will stop the play.*

(e) When either team is below the numerical strength of its opponent and a player of the team of greater numerical strength causes a stoppage of play by striking the puck with his stick above the height of his shoulder, the resulting face-off shall be made at one of the end face-off spots adjacent to the goal of the team causing the stoppage.

Rule 59.　　　Holding an Opponent

A minor penalty shall be imposed on a player who holds an opponent with hands or stick or in any other way.

Rule 60.　　　　　Hooking

(a) A minor penalty shall be imposed on a player who impedes or seeks to impede the progress of an opponent by "hooking" with his stick.

(b) A major penalty shall be imposed on any player who injures an opponent by "hooking."

When a major penalty is imposed under this rule for a foul resulting in injury to the face or head of an opponent, an automatic fine of twenty-five dollars ($25.00) shall also be imposed.

(NOTE) *When a player is checking another in such a way that there is only stick-to-stick contact such action is NOT either hooking or holding.*

Rule 61.　　　　Icing the Puck

(a) For the purpose of this rule, the center line will divide the ice into halves. Should any player of a team, equal or superior in numerical strength to the opposing team, shoot, bat, or deflect the puck from his own half of the ice, beyond the goal line of the opposing team, play shall be stopped and the puck faced off at the end face-off spot of the offending team, unless on the play the puck shall have entered the net of the opposing team, in which case the goal shall be allowed.

(NOTE 1) *If during the period of a delayed whistle due to a foul by a player of the side NOT in possession, the side in possession "ices" the puck then the face-off following the stoppage of play shall take place in the Neutral Zone near the Defending Blue Line of the team "icing" the puck.*

(NOTE 2) *When a team is "short-handed" as the result of a penalty and the penalty is about to expire, the decision as to whether there has been an "icing" shall be determined at the instant the penalty expires, and if the puck crosses the opponents' goal line after the penalty has expired it is "icing." The action of the penalized player remaining in the penalty box will not alter the ruling.*

(NOTE 3) *For the purpose of interpretation of this rule "Icing the Puck" is completed the instant the puck is touched first by a defending player (other than the goalkeeper) after it has crossed the Goal Line and if in the action of so touching the puck it is knocked or deflected into the net it is NO goal.*

(NOTE 4) *When the puck is shot and rebounds from the body or stick of an opponent in his own half of the ice so as to cross the goal line of the player shooting it shall* not *be considered as "icing."*

(NOTE 5) *Notwithstanding the provisions of this section concerning "batting" the puck in respect to the "icing the puck" rule, the provisions of the final paragraph of Rule 57 (e) apply and NO goal can be scored by batting the puck with the hand into the opponents goal whether attended or not.*

(NOTE 6) *If while the Linesman has signalled a slow whistle for a clean interception under Rule 71 (c), the player intercepting shoots or bats the puck beyond the opponent's goal line in such a manner as to constitute "icing the puck," the Linesman's "slow whistle" shall be considered exhausted the instant the puck crosses the blue line and "icing" shall be called in the usual manner.*

(b) If a player of the side shooting the puck down the ice who is on-side and eligible to play the puck does so before it is touched by an opposing player, the play shall continue and it shall not be considered a violation of this rule.

(c) If the puck was so shot by a player of a side below the numerical strength of the opposing team, play shall continue and the face-off shall not take place.

(d) If, however, the puck shall go beyond the goal line in the opposite half of the ice directly from either of the players while facing off, it shall not be considered a violation of the rule.

(e) If, in the opinion of the Linesman, a player of the opposing team excepting the goalkeeper is able to play the puck before it passes his goal line, but has not done so, the face-off shall not be allowed, and play shall continue. If, in the opinion of the Referee, the defending side intentionally abstains from playing the puck promptly when they are in a position to do so, he shall stop the play and order the resulting face-off on the adjacent corner face-off spot nearest the goal of the team at fault.

(NOTE) *The purpose of this section is to enforce continuous action and both Referee and Linesmen should interpret and apply the rule to produce this result.*

(f) If the puck shall touch any part of a player of the opposing side or his skates or his stick, or if it passes through any part of the goal crease before it shall have reached his goal line, or shall have touched the goalkeeper or his skates or his stick at any time before or after crossing his goal line it shall not be considered as "icing the puck" and play shall continue.

(NOTE) *If the goaltender takes any action to dislodge the puck from back of the nets the icing shall be washed out.*

(g) If the Linesman shall have erred in calling an "icing the puck" infraction (regardless of whether either team is short-handed) the puck shall be faced on the center ice face-off spot.

Rule 62.   Interference

(a) A minor penalty shall be imposed on a player who interferes with or impedes the progress of an opponent who is not in possession of the puck, or who deliberately knocks a stick out of an opponent's hand or who prevents a player who has dropped his stick from regaining possession of it or who knocks or shoots any abandoned or broken stick or illegal puck or other debris towards an opposing puck carrier in a manner that could cause him to be distracted.

(NOTE) *The last player to touch the puck—other than a goalkeeper—shall be considered the player in possession. In interpreting this rule the Referee should make sure which of the players is the one creating the interference—Often it is the action and movement of the attacking player which causes the interference since the defending players are entitled to "stand their ground" or "shadow" the attacking players. Players of the side in possession shall not be allowed to "run" deliberate interference for the puck carrier.*

(b) A minor penalty shall be imposed on any player on the players' bench or on the penalty bench who by means of his stick or his body interferes with the movements of the puck or of any opponent on the ice during the progress of play.

(c) A minor penalty shall be imposed on a player who, by means of his stick or his body, interferes with or impedes the movements of the goalkeeper by actual physical contact, while he is in his goal crease area unless the puck is already in that area.

(d) Unless the puck is in the goal crease area, a player of the attacking side not in possession may not stand on the goal crease line or in the goal crease or hold his stick in the goal crease area, and if the puck should enter the net while such condition prevails, a goal shall not be allowed, and the puck shall be faced in the neutral zone at face-off spot nearest the attacking zone of the offending team.

(e) If a player of the attacking side has been physically interfered with by the action of any defending player so as to cause him to be in the goal crease, and the puck should enter the net while the player so interfered with, is still within the goal crease, the

"goal" shall be allowed.

(f) If when the goalkeeper has been removed from the ice any member of his team not legally on the ice including the Manager, Coach or Trainer interferes by means of his body or stick or any other object with the movements of the puck or an opposing player, the Referee shall immediately award a goal to the non-offending team.

(NOTE) *The attention of Referees is directed particularly to three types of offensive interference which should be penalized;*

(1) *When the defending team secures possession of the puck in its own end and the other players of that team run interference for the puck carrier by forming a protective screen against forecheckers;*

(2) *When a player facing off obstructs his opposite number after the face-off when the opponent is not in possession of the puck;*

(3) *When the puck carrier makes a drop pass and follows through so as to make bodily contact with an opposing player.*

Defensive interference consists of bodily contact with an opposing player who is not in possession of the puck.

Rule 63.   Interference by Spectators

(a) In the event of a player being held or interfered with by a spectator, the Referee or Linesman shall blow the whistle and play shall be stopped, unless the team of the player interfered with is in possession of the puck at this time when the play shall be allowed to be completed before blowing the whistle, and the puck shall be faced at the spot where last played at time of stoppage.

(NOTE) *The Referee shall report to the President for disciplinary action, all cases in which a player becomes involved in an altercation with a spectator but no penalty should be imposed.*

(b) In the event that objects are thrown on the ice which interfere with the progress of the game the Referee shall blow the whistle and stop the play, and the puck shall be faced-off at the spot play is stopped.

Rule 64.   Kicking Player

A match penalty shall be imposed on any player who kicks or attempts to kick another player, but a substitute shall be permitted at the end of the fifth minute.

(NOTE) *When actual injury results this foul may be penalized also as a deliberate injury under Rule 49.*

Rule 65.   Kicking Puck

Kicking the puck shall be permitted in all zones, but a goal may not be scored by the kick of an attacking player except if an attacking player kicks the puck and it is deflected into the net by any players of the defending side except the goalkeeper.

Rule 66.   Leaving Players' Bench or Penalty Bench

(a) No player may leave the players' bench at any time to enter an altercation, but substitutions shall be permitted provided the players so substituting do not enter the altercation.

Likewise no player on or near the players' bench (not on the ice) shall participate in any fight or other altercation with any opposing player on the ice.

(b) For infringement of this rule an automatic fine of fifty dollars ($50.00) shall be imposed on each player so infringing the rule. The Referee shall report all such infractions to the President who shall have full power to impose such further penalty as he shall deem fitting.

(NOTE) *This automatic fine shall be imposed in addition to the normal penalties imposed for fouls committed by the player after he has left the players' bench.*

(c) Except at the end of each period, or on expiration of penalty, no player may at any time leave the penalty bench.

(d) A penalized player who leaves the penalty bench before his penalty has expired, whether play is in progress or not, but does not enter an altercation, shall incur an additional minor penalty, after serving his unexpired penalty.

(e) Any penalized player leaving the penalty bench during stoppage of play, and entering an altercation, shall incur a minor penalty plus a ten-minute misconduct penalty, after serving his unexpired time, and an automatic fine of twenty-five dollars ($25.00).

(f) If a player leaves the penalty bench before his penalty is fully served, the Penalty Timekeeper shall note the time and signal the Referee who will immediately stop the play.

(g) In the case of player returning to the ice before his time has expired through an error of the Penalty Timekeeper, he is not to serve an additional penalty, but must serve his unexpired time.

(h) If a player of an attacking side in possession of the puck shall be in such a position as to have no opposition between him and the opposing goalkeeper, and while in such position he shall be interfered with by a player of the opposing side who shall have illegally entered the game, the Referee shall award a penalty shot against the side to which the offending player belongs.

(i) If the opposing goalkeeper has been removed and an attacking player in possession of the puck shall have no player of the defending team to pass and a stick or a part thereof is thrown by an opposing player or the player is fouled from behind thereby being prevented from having a clear shot on an open goal, a goal shall be awarded against the offending team.

If when the opposing goalkeeper has been removed from the ice a player of the side attacking the unattended goal is interfered with by a player who shall have entered the game illegally, the Referee shall immediately award a goal to the non-offending team.

(j) Any Coach who gets on the ice after the start of a period or before the finish of any game, shall be automatically fined fifty dollars ($50.00).

(k) Any Club Executive or Manager committing the same offense, will be automatically fined one hundred dollars ($100.00).

(l) If a penalized player returns to the ice from the penalty bench before his penalty has expired by his own error or the error of the Penalty Timekeeper, any goal scored by his own team while he is illegally on the ice shall be disallowed, but all penalties imposed on either team shall be served as regular penalties.

(m) If a player shall illegally enter the game from his own players' bench, any goal scored by his own team while he is illegally on the ice shall be disallowed, but all penalties imposed against either team shall be served as regular penalties.

Rule 67. Molesting Officials

(a) Any player who touches or holds a Referee, Linesman or any game official, with his hand or his stick or trips or body-checks any of such officials, shall automatically receive a ten-minute penalty for misconduct for the first offense, and a game misconduct penalty for a second offense, in the same game. The use of a substitute for the player so suspended shall be permitted.

(b) Any Club Executive, Manager, Coach or Trainer who holds or strikes an official, shall be automatically suspended from the game, ordered to the dressing room, and a substantial fine shall be imposed by the President.

Rule 68. Obscene or Profane Language or Gestures

(a) Players shall not use obscene or profane language or gestures on the ice or anywhere in the rink. For violation of this rule a misconduct penalty shall be imposed except where the violation occurs in the vicinity of the players' bench in which case a bench minor penalty shall be imposed.

(b) Club Executives, Managers, Coaches and Trainers shall not use obscene or profane language or gestures anywhere in the rink. For violation of this rule a bench minor penalty shall be imposed.

(NOTE) *It is the responsibility of all game officials and all Club officials to send a confidential report to the President setting out the full details concerning the use of obscene gestures by any player, coach or other official. The President shall take such further disciplinary action as he shall deem appropriate.*

Rule 69 Off-Sides

(a) The position of the player's skates and not that of his stick shall be the determining factor in all instances in deciding an "off-side." A player is off-side when both skates are completely over the outer edge of the determining center line or blue line involved in the play.

(NOTE 1) *A player is "on-side" when "either" of his skates are in contact with or on his own side of the line at the instant the puck completely crosses the outer edge of that line regardless of the position of his stick.*

(NOTE 2) *It should be noted that while the position of the player's skates is what determines whether a player is "off-side" nevertheless the question of "off-side" never arises until the puck has completely crossed the outer edge of the line at which time the decision is to be made.*

(b) If in the opinion of the Linesman an intentional off-side play has been made, the puck shall be faced-off at the end face-off spot in the defending zone of the offending team.

(NOTE 3) *This rule does not apply to a team below the numerical strength of its opponent. In such cases the puck shall be faced-off at the spot from which the pass was made.*

(NOTE 4) *An intentional off-side is one which is made for the purpose of securing a stoppage of play regardless of the reason, or where an off-side play is made under conditions where there is no possibility of completing a legal pass.*

Rule 70. Passes

(a) The puck may be passed by any player to a player of the same side within any one of the three zones into which the ice is divided, but may not be passed forward from a player in one zone to a player of the same side in another zone, except by a player on the defending team, who may make and take forward passes from their own defending zone to the center line without incurring an off-side penalty. This "forward pass" from the defending zone must be completed by the pass receiver who is legally on-side at the center line.

(NOTE 1) *The position of the puck (not the player's skates) shall be the determining factor in deciding from which zone the pass was made.*

(NOTE 2) *Passes may be completed legally at the center red line in exactly the same manner as passes at the attacking blue line.*

(b) Should the puck, having been passed, contact any part of the body, stick or skates of a player of the same side who is legally on-side, the pass shall be considered to have been completed.

(c) The player last touched by the puck shall be deemed to be in possession.

Rebounds off goalkeeper's pads or other equipment shall not be considered as a change of possession or the completion of the play by the team when applying Rule 34 (b).

(d) If a player in the Neutral Zone is preceded into the Attacking Zone by the puck passed from the Neutral Zone he shall be eligible to take possession of the puck anywhere in the Attacking Zone except when the "Icing the Puck" rule applies.

(e) If a player in the same zone from which a pass is made is preceded by the puck into succeeding zones he shall be eligible to take possession of the puck in that zone except where the "Icing the Puck" rule applies.

(f) If an attacking player passes the puck backward toward his own goal from the Attacking Zone, an opponent may play the puck anywhere regardless of whether he (the opponent) was in the same zone at the time the puck was passed or not. *(No "slow whistle").*

Rule 71.   Preceding Puck into Attacking Zone

(a) Players of an attacking team must not precede the puck into the Attacking Zone.

(b) For violation of this rule, the play is stopped, and puck shall be faced-off in the Neutral Zone at face-off spot nearest the Attacking Zone of the offending team.

(NOTE) *A player actually propelling the puck who shall cross the line ahead of the puck, shall not be considered "off-side."*

(c) If, however, notwithstanding the fact that a member of the attacking team shall have preceded the puck into the Attacking Zone, the puck be cleanly intercepted by a member of the defending team at or near the blue line, and be carried or passed by them into the Neutral Zone the "off-side" shall be ignored and play permitted to continue.

(Officials will carry out this rule by means of the "slow whistle").

(d) If a player legally carries or passes the puck from the Neutral Zone back into his own Defending Zone while a player of the opposing team is in such Defending Zone, the "off-side" shall be ignored and play permitted to continue.
(No "slow whistle").

Rule 72.   Puck Out of Bounds or Unplayable

(a) When the puck goes outside the playing area at either end, or either side of the rink or strikes any obstacles above the playing surface other than the boards, glass or wire it shall be faced-off from whence it was shot or deflected, unless otherwise expressly provided in these rules.

(b) When the puck becomes lodged in the netting on the outside of either goal so as to make it unplayable, or if it is frozen between opposing players intentionally or otherwise, the Referee shall stop the play and face-off the puck at either of the adjacent face-off spots unless in the opinion of the Referee the stoppage was caused by a player of the attacking team, in which case the resulting face-off shall be conducted in the Neutral Zone.

(NOTE) *This includes stoppage of play caused by player of attacking side shooting the puck on to the back of the defending team's net without any intervening action by the defending team.*

The defending team and/or the attacking team may play the puck off the net at any time. However,

should the puck remain on the net for longer than three seconds, play shall be stopped and the face-off shall take place in the end face-off zone except when the stoppage is caused by the attacking team, then the face-off shall take place on a face-off spot in the neutral zone.

(c) A minor penalty shall be imposed on a goalkeeper who deliberately drops the puck on the goal netting to cause a stoppage of play.

(d) If the puck comes to rest on top of the boards surrounding the playing area it shall be considered to be in play and may be played legally by hand or stick.

Rule 73.   Puck Must Be Kept in Motion

(a) The puck must at all times be kept in motion.

(b) Except to carry the puck behind its goal once, a side in possession of the puck in its own defense area shall always advance the puck towards the opposing goal, except if it shall be prevented from so doing by players of the opposing side.

For the first infraction of this rule play shall be stopped and a face-off shall be made at either end face-off spot adjacent to the goal of the team causing the stoppage, and the Referee shall warn the Captain or Alternate Captain of the offending team of the reason for the face-off. For a second violation by any player of the same team in the same period a minor penalty shall be imposed on the player violating the rule.

(c) A minor penalty shall also be imposed on any player who deliberately holds the puck against the boards in any manner unless he is being checked by an opponent.

(d) A player beyond his defense area shall not pass nor carry the puck backward into his Defense Zone for the purpose of delaying the game except when his team is below the numerical strength of the opponents on the ice.

(e) For an infringement of this rule, the face-off shall be at the nearest end face-off spot in the Defending Zone of the offending team.

Rule 74.   Puck Out of Sight and Illegal Puck

(a) Should a scramble take place, or a player accidentally fall on the puck, and the puck be out of sight of the Referee, he shall immediately blow his whistle and stop the play. The puck shall then be "faced-off" at the point where the play was stopped, unless otherwise provided for in the rules.

(b) If, at any time while play is in progress a puck other than the one legally in play shall appear on the playing surface, the play shall not be stopped but shall continue with the legal puck until the play then in progress is completed by change of possession.

Rule 75.   Puck Striking Official

Play shall not be stopped if the puck touches an official anywhere on the rink, regardless of whether a team is short-handed or not.

Rule 76.   Refusing to Start Play

(a) If, when both teams are on the ice, one team for any reason shall refuse to play when ordered to do so by the Referee, he shall warn the Captain or Alternate Captain and allow the team so refusing fifteen seconds within which to begin the game or resume play. If at the end of that time the team shall still refuse to play, the Referee shall impose a two-minute penalty on a player of the offending team to be designated by the Manager or Coach of that team, through the playing Captain; and should there be a repetition of the same incident the Referee shall notify the Manager or Coach that he has been fined the sum of one hundred dollars ($100.00), and should there be a recurrence of the same incident, the Referee shall have no alternative but to declare that the game be forfeited to the non-offending club, and the case shall be reported to the President for further action.

(b) If a team, when ordered to do so by the Referee, through its Club Executive, Manager or Coach, fails to go on the ice, and start play within five minutes, the Club Executive, Manager or Coach shall be fined five hundred dollars ($500.00); the game shall be forfeited, and the case shall be reported to the President for further action.

(NOTE) *The President of the League shall issue instructions pertaining to records, etc., of a forfeited game.*

Rule 77. Slashing

(a) A minor or major penalty, at the discretion of the Referee, shall be imposed on any player who impedes or seeks to impede the progress of an opponent by "slashing" with his stick.

(b) A major penalty shall be imposed on any player who injures an opponent by slashing. When a major penalty is imposed under this rule for a foul resulting in injury to the face or head of an opponent, an automatic fine of twenty-five dollars ($25.00) shall also be imposed.

(NOTE) *Referees should penalize as "slashing" any player who swings his stick at any opposing player (whether in or out of range) without actually striking him or where a player on the pretext of playing the puck makes a wild swing at the puck with the object of intimidating an opponent.*

(c) Any player who swings his stick at another player in the course of any altercation shall be subject to a fine of not less than two hundred dollars ($200), with or without suspension, to be imposed by the President.

(NOTE) *The Referee shall impose the normal appropriate penalty provided in the other sections of this rule and shall in addition report promptly to the President all infractions under this section.*

Rule 78. Spearing

(a) A minor or major penalty, at the discretion of the Referee, shall be imposed on a player who spears or attempts to spear an opponent. Every penalty under this rule shall include an automatic fine of twenty-five dollars ($25.00).

(NOTE) *"Attempt to spear" shall include all cases where a spearing gesture is made regardless of whether bodily contact is made or not.*

(b) A major penalty shall be imposed on a player who spears a goalkeeper while the goalkeeper is within his goal crease.

(c) A major penalty shall be imposed on any player who injures an opponent by spearing.

When a major penalty is imposed under this rule for a foul resulting in injury to the face or head of an opponent, an automatic fine of twenty-five dollars ($25.00) shall also be imposed.

"Spearing" shall mean stabbing an opponent with the point of the stick blade while the stick is being carried with one hand or both hands.

Spearing may also be treated as a "deliberate attempt to injure" under Rule 44.

Rule 79. Start of Game and Periods

(a) The game shall be commenced at the time scheduled by a "face-off" in the center of the rink and shall be renewed promptly at the conclusion of each intermission in the same manner.

No delay shall be permitted by reason of any

ceremony, exhibition, demonstration or presentation unless consented to reasonably in advance by the visiting team.

(b) Home clubs shall have the choice of goals to defend at the start of the game except where both players' benches are on the same side of the rink, in which case the home club shall start the game defending the goal nearest to its own bench. The teams shall change ends for each succeeding regular or overtime period.

(c) During the pre-game warm-up and before the commencement of play in any period each team shall confine its activity to its own end of the rink so as to leave clear an area thirty feet wide across the center of the Neutral Zone.

(d) Fifteen minutes before the time scheduled for the start of the game both teams shall vacate the ice and proceed to their dressing rooms while the ice is being flooded. Both teams shall be signalled by the Game Timekeeper to return to the ice together in time for the scheduled start of the game.

(e) When a team fails to appear on the ice promptly without proper justification a fine shall be assessed against the offending team. The amount of the fine to be decided by the President.

Rule 80. Throwing Stick

(a) When any player of the defending side, including the goalkeeper, deliberately throws his stick or any part thereof or any other object, at the puck in his Defending Zone, the Referee shall allow the play to be completed and if a goal is not scored a penalty shot shall be awarded to the non-offending side, which shot shall be taken by the player designated by the Referee as the player fouled.

If, however, the goal being unattended and the attacking player having no defending player to pass and having a chance to score on an "open net," a stick or part thereof or any other object, be thrown by a defending player thereby preventing a shot on the "open net" a goal shall be awarded to the attacking side.

(b) A major penalty shall be imposed on any player who throws his stick or any part thereof or any other object, in any zone, except when such act has been penalized by the award of a penalty shot or a goal.

(NOTE) *When a player discards the broken portion of a stick by tossing it to the side of the ice (and not over the boards) in such a way as will not interfere with play or opposing player, no penalty will be imposed for so doing.*

(c) The Referee and Linesmen shall report promptly to the President for disciplinary action every case where a stick or any part thereof is thrown outside the playing area.

Rule 81. Time of Match

(a) The time allowed for a game shall be three twenty-minute periods of actual play with a rest intermission between periods.

Play shall be resumed promptly following each intermission upon the expiry of fifteen minutes from the completion of play in the preceding period. A preliminary warning shall be given by the Game Timekeeper to the officials and to both teams three minutes prior to the resumption of play in each period and the final warning shall be given in sufficient time to enable the teams to resume play promptly.

(b) The team scoring the greatest number of goals during the three twenty-minute periods shall be the winner, and shall be credited with two points in the League standing.

(c) In the intervals between periods, the ice surface shall be flooded unless mutually agreed to the contrary.

(d) If any unusual delay occurs within five minutes of the end of the first or second periods the Referee may order the next regular intermission to be taken immediately and the balance of the period will be completed on the resumption of play with the teams defending the same goals, after which the teams will change ends and resume play of the ensuing period without delay.

Rule 82. Tied Games

(a) If, at the end of the three regular twenty-minute periods, the score shall be tied, the game shall be called a "TIE," and each team shall be credited with one point in the League standing.

(b) Special conditions for duration and number of periods of play-off games, shall be arranged by the Board of Governors.

Rule 83. Tripping

(a) A minor penalty shall be imposed on any player who shall place his stick, knee, foot, arm, hand or elbow in such a manner that it shall cause his opponent to trip or fall.

(NOTE 1) *If in the opinion of the Referee a player is unquestionably hook-checking the puck and obtains possession of it, thereby tripping puck carrier, no penalty shall be imposed.*

(b) When a player, in control of the puck in the Attacking Zone, and having no other opponent to pass than the goalkeeper, is tripped or otherwise fouled from behind thus preventing a reasonable scoring opportunity a penalty shot shall be awarded to the non-offending side. Nevertheless the Referee shall not stop the play until the attacking side has lost possession of the puck to the defending side.

(NOTE 2) *The intention of this rule is to restore a reasonable scoring opportunity which has been lost by reason of a foul from behind when the foul is committed in the Attacking Zone.*

By "control of the puck" is meant the act of propelling the puck with the stick. If while it is being propelled the puck is touched by another player or his equipment or hits the goal or goes free the player shall no longer be considered to be "in control of the puck."

(c) If, when the opposing goalkeeper has been removed from the ice, a player in control of the puck is tripped or otherwise fouled with no opposition between him and the opposing goal, thus preventing a reasonable scoring opportunity, the Referee shall immediately stop the play and award a goal to the attacking team.

Rule 84. Unnecessary Roughness

At the discretion of the Referee, a minor penalty may be imposed on any player deemed guilty of unnecessary roughness.

COLLEGIATE RULES DIFFERENCES

Except for the colleges, the amateur and professional leagues of the United States and Canada follow the National Hockey League (NHL) rules just detailed. Some of the leagues, of course, have minor differences, but the basic rules are the same. Only the collegiate rules and those used in international competitions such as the Olympic Games and the International Ice Hockey Federation tournament vary to any degree.

Since, in college hockey, there is no center red line, there are the following differences in rules:

In college hockey, icing is called when the puck is shot the length of the rink from inside the defensive blue line; by NHL rules, the center red line is the determining factor. In the colleges, a player can pass from his own end all the way to his opponent's blue line; by NHL rules, that pass over two lines is offside. The colleges also call icing against a shorthanded team, do not permit body-checking in the attacking (offensive) zone, and fighting means expulsion from the game.